Feb 2006

Bill —
Hope you enjoy! The physical
trials are almost like Iron Man!

Jeff Turai

BEYOND
THE
SUMMIT

BEYOND
THE
SUMMIT

Setting and Surpassing
Extraordinary Business Goals

TODD SKINNER

PORTFOLIO

PORTFOLIO

Published by the Penguin Group

Penguin Group (USA) Inc., 375 Hudson Street, New York, New York 10014, U.S.A.
Penguin Books Ltd, 80 Strand, London WC2R 0RL, England
Penguin Books Australia Ltd, 250 Camberwell Road, Camberwell, Victoria 3124, Australia
Penguin Books Canada Ltd, 10 Alcorn Avenue, Toronto, Ontario, Canada M4V 3B2
Penguin Books India (P) Ltd, 11 Community Centre, Panchsheel Park, New Delhi–110 017, India
Penguin Books (N.Z.) Ltd, Cnr Rosedale and Airborne Roads, Albany, Auckland, New Zealand
Penguin Books (South Africa) (Pty) Ltd, 24 Sturdee Avenue, Rosebank, Johannesburg 2196, South Africa

Penguin Books Ltd, Registered Offices: 80 Strand, London WC2R 0RL, England

First published in 2003 by Portfolio, a member of Penguin Group (USA) Inc.

10 9 8 7 6 5 4 3 2 1

LIBRARY OF CONGRESS CATALOGING-IN-PUBLICATION DATA
Skinner, Todd.
    Beyond the summit : setting and surpassing extraordinary business goals / Todd
Skinner.
        p.   cm.
    Includes index.
    ISBN 1-59184-004-X
    1. Management by objectives.   2. Strategic planning.   3. Success in business.
4. Mountaineering—Psychological aspects.   I. Title.
HD30.65.S55   2003
658.4'012—dc21   2003051708

This book is printed on acid-free paper. ∞

Printed in the United States of America

ACKNOWLEDGMENTS

My sister, Holly Skinner, acted as coauthor of this book and is the finest wordsmith I know. Her award-winning book *Eye of the Blackbird: A Story of Gold in the American West* is an adventure in itself and I highly recommend it.

I would also like to acknowledge my climbing partners past and present who never get the credit they deserve, and thank the many kindred spirits who have given encouragement and help on my ascent.

CONTENTS

INTRODUCTION

I might have dedicated this book to Wyoming's Wind River Mountains—my earliest and most influential teachers—for it was there I first began to understand the profound transformative power of great challenges. When I stood on my first summit at the age of eleven, what I could see was mountains all around me, and more mountains beyond me: beautiful, sunlit granite ramparts all beckoning me to climb them as well.

Even then I realized I could not climb them all, and I would have to find a way to choose among them. And I knew I wasn't a good-enough climber yet to reach the summit of those I did choose. But I found that the mountains themselves have the power to make us good enough—the challenge encourages us to rise to meet it, and each mountain prepares us to climb the next.

After more than thirty years of aspiring to reach the most challenging summits all over the world, I am still finding mountains that are beyond me, choosing among them for which will give me the greatest capacity to climb farther, and discovering strategies that improved my success not just in climbing, but in every other endeavor. The rare and valuable lessons I have brought back from the mountains are presented here for the climber in us all, because mountains provide a natural metaphor for challenging goals in both business and life.

In 1989, when I first began to speak about what mountains have taught me, it was to audiences of outdoor and climbing enthusiasts; but I was soon recruited by forward-thinking corporations because I was seen as an extreme innovator in my field. I still remember the first time I stood in front of that new audience—a very successful, world-renowned, cutting-edge technology company—with five thousand faces looking up at me. They probably were wondering what a rock climber could tell them about business. I was wondering how to translate my world to theirs, how I could illustrate the parallels I knew they would find useful, and explain my passion for seeking higher ground.

I found to my amazement that they didn't need a translation, because we spoke the same language. They already thought like first ascensionists—they saw immediately how a storm on the mountain was like a downturn in the economy, that crevasses are business pitfalls, and difficult terrain requires the same problem-solving skills no matter where that terrain is. Our common ground was an elevated field of endeavor, the very nature of the quest. They knew what it felt like to stand below an audacious mountain, to pursue improbable goals, and how the most compelling journeys begin where the map ends.

I was rewarded at the end of the presentation with my first standing ovation. Many individuals came up to me afterward to tell me about storms or crevasses they had faced in their respective fields, and I was surprised at the variety of ways they had interpreted and planned to use the lessons I had offered. I saw then that it was much better to let them make their own connections to what I had found to be true in the high mountains. I will let you make the connections to your own personal climbs as well, for wherever we are, even on flat ground, there are mountains all around us.

To successfully climb a mountain or to succeed at any endeavor, you must know how to define your objective, choose the best team for that objective and prepare for the unknown, make the critical transition from preparation to action, cross up and over difficult terrain, weather the storms well, and go the distance to the summit to complete your objective.

This book contains essential strategies to help you navigate through that journey. And while they are distilled from my experiences on real mountains, they are designed to be applied to any kind of challenge you undertake, and have been successfully incorporated by the many intrepid individuals, and companies, who have also asked me to speak about our parallel journeys of ascent.

BEYOND
THE
SUMMIT

1. THE MOUNTAIN

Why Climb?

This book began at 19,500 feet, dangling on the side of a rocket-shaped mountain I was told could not be climbed, fifty-eight days into an ascent I thought would take fifteen. I was sitting, exhausted, in the door of an unstable hanging tent pinned by one anchor to the sheer wall, my feet swinging out over two thousand feet of thin air. My shredded hands were bleeding through layers of protective tape, and my lips and ears had been scalded and blistered by the unfiltered sun. I watched the haunted faces of my teammates, swinging on ropes to chip ice to melt for water, looking to gauge what reserves they might have left. After months in this killing altitude, our strength was decimated, the food and fuel we came with was almost gone, and we were the last climbers still alive in the most deadly season in Karakoram history.

Surrounded by clouds, curling in tendrils around peak after endless peak to the darkened horizon, with drifting flakes of snow a reminder that the Himalayan winter had arrived, I felt compelled to think about the mountains that had led me to this far point. They had been improbable mountains, even impossible, some had thought—not pyramid mountains but parabolic, their sheared-off faces thousands of feet high, steep beyond vertical and seeming to defy ascent using only hands and feet. I began to study why, against all odds, I had succeeded on those mountains. And why, on this mountain, I was so close to failing.

I had crossed half the world, trekked through the most precipitous terrain on earth, fought my way up a vertical mile of mountain, and had only 350 feet that remained to be climbed to reach this mountain's summit. But I did not know if what remained could be climbed. All the decisions we make on an expedition affect the outcome, and I pondered if there was something I could have done differently to make this outcome less uncertain. Did I make the right choices yesterday? Ten days earlier? Ten years ago? What, I wondered, leads to success? What, in fact, is the definition of success? How can the balance between success and failure teeter as precariously as the hanging tent I was perched on?

If I could finally distill the lessons that each mountain had taught me, I would have a guidebook to bring with me for all mountains. That guidebook wouldn't be a compendium of answers, but a set of strategies to help find answers in unknown terrain. It would identify the hazards and obstacles in any ascent, and discover ways to navigate through those obstacles. It would list the essentials you need to carry in your backpack when venturing into the frontier, and, just as important, what you essentially need to leave behind.

As the Himalayan night closed in with its cold and hostile embrace, I thought about strategies that would help me tomorrow, and would still be helping me twenty years from tomorrow. After that night I continued to think, to distill, to test and revise, to construct a strategic framework for success when you are facing the unknown, and this book is the end result. The last question I might have asked myself that dark and frigid night was: "Why was I here?" But that answer I already knew.

I was here because I heard that it was the highest freestanding spire and potentially most challenging free climb in the world—a dagger of golden granite rising 20,500 feet into the frozen sky of the Karakoram Himalayas. On the west side lay Pakistan and the border of Afghanistan. To the southeast stretched India, Nepal, and

Tibet, and directly east China staggered with mountains unnamed and unclimbed. The daunting east face of Trango Tower was ominously steep and sheer, with thin cracks and tiny ledges barely discernible along its rising face. The Himalayan experts, those who had been on Everest and nearby K2, doubted it could be climbed using only hands and feet, and at first I had no reason to question their disbelief.

The obstacles seemed overwhelming. At altitudes above eighteen thousand feet, you begin to die from oxygen deprivation, which inhibits the rebuilding of muscle. Even walking becomes difficult in such rarefied air, and gymnastic climbing is much more like a sprint. The thin atmosphere transmits searing heat in daylight, and numbing cold in shadow and darkness. Uncontrollable rock and ice fall are a constant menace in this environment, avalanches sweep down without warning, and the fierce Himalayan storms are frequently deadly.

The rock itself on Trango was a beautiful Karakoram granite, the climbing features perfect and beckoning, but the sustained difficulty made it the most technically challenging mountain I could find in any range on any continent. Unlike other better-known and often-climbed Himalayan peaks, it had no long snow ridges and sloping ascents, but rocketed up three thousand straight feet, like three Empire State Buildings stacked on top of each other, three hundred stories and no elevator.

So when the Polish climber Voytek Kurtyka first showed me a picture of the east face of Trango Tower and said I should go to climb it, I just laughed. But he was serious. It's not that he thought I *could* climb it; he didn't. But he thought this mountain represented the future of climbing, and I was the person best poised to begin the journey into that future. I had climbed the four most difficult big walls in North America, each of which could have been the goal of a lifetime.* I had won the American Alpine Club's prestigious Underhill Award for climbing achievement, and was

---

*The climbs are described in Paul Piana's *Big Walls: Breakthroughs on the Free Climbing Frontier* (Sierra Club, 1997).

recognized as one of the best rock climbers in the world. In theory I could have been content to rest on my laurels.

Why should I travel halfway around the world, pulling a team and tons of gear with me, to attempt an ascent of a mountain so obviously impossible to climb? What could I gain from it? How could I risk so much when I didn't really have to? But the idea of Trango Tower stayed in my mind, a knife blade of stone whose edge I could almost feel, and I began to think of it not so much as impossible, but as ultimate, the most difficult challenge I could undertake. And that was reason enough to try.

Trango Tower was more than just a mountain. It represented who I could become. Aspiration is one of the qualities that most defines us: who we want to be, where we want to go. Our real greatness lies in this desire to move higher, to step beyond where we are. It is both an individual impulse and the motivation behind a great team, whether that team is a partnership, a company, or a nation. We are always in the process of becoming—setting goals, defining values, delineating landmarks where we would like to arrive.

We are all climbers because we have this innate desire to rise, to improve our lives, to succeed at our endeavors. The real question is how do we achieve that rise and increase the odds of our success? To answer that question for myself, I had to develop a strategy of movement, a framework for making choices that could answer the question "What should my next step be in order to increase my level of success?" I realized that if you take the element of luck out of the equation of success, and in most cases luck plays a minuscule role, then success becomes a matter of making correct decisions. The right choice moves us forward, and the wrong choice sets us back. (Even hard work, which we often consider an essential component of success, is a decision to work hard.) But how do we know what the correct decisions are?

In a simplified example, you come to a crossroad that requires you to choose the left or right fork. Which way do you turn? Your answer depends entirely on your intended destination. Where is it you want to go? Using the information you have, you choose the fork that is most likely to lead to your destination. If your destination is vague ("I want to go far . . ."), it is much harder to make the correct decisions because you can't begin to guess which turns lead there. If every decision you make is based on a well-defined destination, you are much more likely to arrive where you want to go.

But destination presupposes a direction. Before we can decide where to go, we need to know why we are going, what we expect to gain from arriving there, and how that arrival will further our continued ascent. I have found that successfully climbing one mountain does not automatically translate to success on the next mountain, or to success in the larger life. It can, in fact, have the opposite effect and be detrimental to future success when we choose the wrong mountain, start out for the wrong reasons, or climb in a way that injures our ability to keep climbing. Every destination has to be placed in a larger context—we are not climbing to a solitary mountain top, but using each mountain as a step up a directed lifelong ascent of enduring success.

So "the next step" toward success is determined by the destination, and destination is determined by direction. While everybody has a different definition of what constitutes success, when you boil it down, success is gaining that which you find valuable. To achieve that gain, you first have to discover what it is that gives you value, which provides direction. Then you choose a destination that will move you in that direction. The destination you have chosen ultimately provides you with the answer of what the next step should be.

In mountain climbing, we refer to the organized effort to reach a defined destination as an expedition. That destination is the summit of the mountain, which might be a dollar amount if you are in sales, a finished book if you are a writer, a time or distance if you are a runner, a well-adjusted and capable child if you are a parent. A challenge of any kind can be thought of as a mountain, when your mission is to successfully complete the endeavor, or overcome a specific problem, and you have a defined destination in mind. Our lives are preoccupied with expeditions of varying difficulty, duration, and reward, and we often juggle many expeditions at once—careers, family, demands of all kinds, each of which requires a conscious strategy to fully succeed on the climb. Expeditions become our primary means of ascent because they provide a destination and demand a strategy to reach that destination, and in the climb we gain what we seek.

Thus my strategy of movement evolved into a *Trinity of Ascent,* made up of the *Climber*—an entity, including any person, company, or group working toward a shared purpose, whose desire is to ascend; the *Expedition*—an organized effort to reach a defined destination; and the *Lifelong Ascent*—a continuum of success that helps you choose mountains by clarifying direction and ensuring each mountain contributes to your further ascent. The primary purpose of the Trinity of Ascent is to increase the gradient of your success by precluding drift, to prevent your life raft from floating aimlessly on the whim of wind and current, to give yourself a compass and a paddle.

To succeed on an expedition, you must think from the summit back, because all decisions are based on the destination. To succeed on your Lifelong Ascent, you must also think from the summit back. If we agree that success is based on making the correct decisions, and that correct decisions are based on arriving at a destination, then we do need an extended destination to be successful in life. I have come to think of that destination as our *Ultimate Potential,* the farthest point of gain on the line of our Lifelong Ascent. It cannot be precisely defined, because that would be self-limiting, but it gives us a theoretical destination to move toward, which elevates our choices and correspondingly our level of success.

Understand that since all your actions affect your future, the future should determine what those actions will be. To gain success, you need a solid framework for making decisions, and this strategy doesn't apply only to an individual person, but to any group endeavor that seeks enduring success. A business without a goal based on its Ultimate Potential must look to the past to decide how far it can go. A team without agreement on a summit works against itself rather than toward a common purpose.

Most of this book is about how to succeed on an expedition by employing conscious strategies to make the correct decisions that allow you to reach a defined destination—lessons I have distilled from the mountains that can be applied to any kind of mountain we set out to climb. But this chapter looks at how to choose mountains that fit on your Lifelong Ascent and move you farthest toward your Ultimate Potential.

1. You are a product of your mountains.

> **Each mountain you climb will change you, and the more challenging the mountain, the more you have to gain from the ascent. Your mountains include not only those you have climbed, but the mountains that others have climbed whose lessons you internalize; and the mountains you dream about climbing, which make you better before you ever set foot on them, and inspire you even if you never set foot on them.**

"All our dreams begin in youth," wrote Heinrich Harrer in *Seven Years in Tibet*, to explain his passion for climbing mountains and exploring strange lands. I found the same passion in my own youth, and it continues to steer my direction and choices. We are all aware of the compass we carry that naturally points toward what we value, giving us at least a sense of direction, but how do we refine that direction to get the most return on our investment? It often seems like direction is a matter of circumstance, dependent on the people and events that have shaped our course along the way. Because outside forces can so powerfully affect us, it is helpful to examine the past to understand what has bumped us on and off course.

When I look back carefully at my own life, I realize much of what I believe and value was influenced at an early age. My father, Bob Skinner, and his five brothers started a wilderness school for youth in the mountains of western Wyoming in 1956, two years before I was born. They taught survival skills, like how to build a shelter in the wilderness when you had none, or a log raft without nails, to navigate wild rivers. But more than anything they taught self-reliance—how to recognize what needed to be done and find a way to do it.

They also taught the fundamentals of climbing mountains. My dad pioneered climbing routes in Yosemite, and British Columbia's Bella Coola Range in the 1950s, while working as a survival instructor for the Air Force. In the mountains, my dad always carried an old army-style backpack that would have killed a modern backpacker—an eighty-pound load slung on a short frame with narrow leather straps over the shoulders and no waist belt, called the "Mountain Mule." I was five or six when I first slid into the harness and tried to stand up. Talk about aspiration!

Every summer my dad or his brother Courtney would lead a month-long expedition to walk the spine of the Wind River Mountains and climb Wyoming's highest, Gannett Peak. I was eleven years old when I first climbed it in a grueling fourteen-hour ascent. While no one that young had ever climbed Gannett, my dad simply assumed I could complete the ascent, and because of his assumption, I could.

While my dad was herculean and pragmatic, Courtney, six years his junior, was a boundless dreamer, and eccentric enough to capture my imagination. Not only did Courtney dream in a way that often didn't adhere to logic or limitations, he had the ability to sell the dreams and make others believe. Pie-in-the-sky ambitions could come true, I found out, and I learned from Courtney to ask, "Why not?"

These two helped shape my youth, one by teaching skill and discipline, and the other the adventure of great dreams, and they illustrate how important heroes can be. We are always seeking the heroic in people, and the more we look for and believe in heroism, that ideal of greatness, the more we are likely to find it. Because we are all in a position to be guides as well as seekers, it is important for us to be mentors to someone else: a nod instead of a frown, the time spent teaching a skill, a hand held out to someone—all can make the difference in a life. We gain most not by reaching our destination, but by bringing others with us on the climb.

While people can affect the course of our lives, experiences are also critical in shaping who we become. The more mountains we climb, the more we learn how to climb successfully. Every challenge, even if it is unpleasant or unwelcome, has something to give us, and rising success is a matter of recognizing the value to be extracted from each climb. What doesn't kill you makes you stronger, they say, or, more accurately, what doesn't kill you has the potential to make you stronger, and after many hazardous undertakings, "I lived to tell about it" is one of my favorite expressions.

The mountains that influence your direction can also include ones that others have climbed, when you learn about them and internalize the inspirations they offer. For example, because my uncle Courtney spent five years in Antarctica with an American research team in the 1960s, I devoured every saga of polar exploration I could find as a kid, like Captain Robert Scott's grueling race to the South Pole. He was beaten there by the Norwegian Roald Amundsen and died of exhaustion on the way back, pinned down by a blizzard only eleven miles from his next supply depot.

And the story of Ernest Shackleton and his mates, whose ship, the *Endurance*, was caught in pack ice and slowly crushed. They were set adrift on floating pack ice that split beneath their feet and lived off seals and the supplies they had salvaged, drifting for six months toward the islands off Patagonia with no chance to be saved by anything but their own tenacity and ingenuity—one of the most gripping adventure tales you could ever read.

But the most horrific story that stayed in my mind was that of Australian Douglas Mawson, who went exploring the inland coast of Antarctica southwest of Australia in 1912. He left his camp at Cape Denison with three dogsleds and two companions. Six weeks and 320 miles out, one companion who was driving the sled with their tent, and all but a week's worth of food, broke through a snow bridge over a crevasse the others had just crossed and disappeared, dogs and all, into the icy abyss.

During Mawson's desperate return voyage, the remaining dogs collapsed one by one and were cooked and eaten as they died. One sled was abandoned, and soon there were no dogs left to pull the second. After three weeks of toil with little food, Mawson's other companion died. Left alone to drag his sled over wind-honed ridges of ice, Mawson began to crawl on his hands and knees. He fell repeatedly into crevasses that split the glacier into shards, saved only by the rope connected to his stubborn sled. After ninety days' absence, Mawson stood unsteadily on the edge of the polar plateau overlooking his camp, only to watch the relief ship that had come to pick him up sail out of the harbor without him.

These were the most grueling experiences I could imagine, and they went a long way toward helping me understand what people are capable of enduring. That insight would serve me in the future, for one of my uncle Courtney's dreams was to stand on top of Gannett Peak on New Year's Day in the first winter ascent of the 13,804-foot mountain. While Gannett is not the highest peak in the Rockies, it is the most alpine in nature, with five glaciers sliding down its sides, and a remote and difficult approach.

Courtney convinced seven of us that his dream could be accomplished, and just after Christmas in 1978, we set off on skis to plow twenty miles into the wilderness dragging hundred-pound sleds. I was nineteen years old and had just finished my third semester of college at the University of Wyoming studying business and finance.

We had actually attempted the climb the year before, but an endless blizzard and minus-fifty-five-degree cold drove us back before we reached the mountain. It was an extreme goal, we all knew, but the magic of a winter Gannett ascent was that it condensed all the elements of a major expedition—the logistics, moving large loads through difficult terrain, a strenuous climb, and a long retreat—into the short frame of ten to twelve days.

To climb Gannett from the western approach involved ascending a steep, thousand-foot-high notch in the dividing rampart, called Bonney Pass, descending that thousand feet to cross a mile-long stretch of crevasse-filled glacier, then climbing up rock and ice two thousand feet to the long snow slope of Gannett's summit. That was the climb I knew in summer.

Winter altered everything. It took us four days to break a trail through twenty miles of deep December snow where lakes were now just levels of white, rocks were mounds of white, and trees were lumps of white. We set our camp on the flank of Bonney Pass where we were out of the avalanche zone, we hoped. Four tents were anchored into the powder, and we dug a snow cave five feet under for our kitchen.

Our climbing window of opportunity was limited by both time and supplies. If the weather was clear at four in the morning, we would set out with a minimum of survival gear, traveling fast and light to make a dash for the mountaintop. In summer it was feasible to cross Bonney Pass, climb Gannett, and come back in the same long day. We thought fast-sliding skis would also make it feasible in winter. So when morning arrived clear and a balmy thirty below under dim starlight, we fixed headlamps over our ski hats and parka hoods, and climbed madly up the steep slope of Bonney Pass. We crested that summit at dawn, skied wildly down the other side, and coasted out onto the glacier only to be stopped dead by chest-deep powder.

We took turns breaking trail through the wallowy snow, moving fifty feet at a time, struggling to press on in our dash that had slowed to a crawl. It took us all day to cross the mile-long bowl of glacier, and when we reached the base of Gannett Peak, it was growing dark again. We had no tents or sleeping bags, only the warm clothes we were wearing, a stove to melt snow for water, and three days of emergency rations. I remembered from summer a large crevasse in the glacier near the mountain's base, and we broke into it from above, crawled onto an ice shelf, lit candles for warmth, and settled in for the night.

The day hadn't gone exactly according to plan, but there was nothing to worry about yet. We wouldn't freeze, we wouldn't starve, and in the morning we would be in position to climb the peak and return along the trail we had already broken. But in the morning it was snowing, and we had to decide whether to go up or go back. Since we had come so far, we decided to go up.

It was another day of floundering through deep snow, struggling upward inches at a time. It began snowing harder, and the long summit ridge in the dim afternoon light seemed to stretch for miles. The visibility was so poor that I passed the summit and nearly stepped off the edge before we realized we were there. We had completed the first winter ascent of Gannett Peak, and after a few minutes celebrating on the summit, we started back in an all-out blizzard.

It was dark again when we reached our bivouac in the crevasse. We crawled in for another cold night while the wind whirled snow above our ice cavern. We cursed the fact that these were some of the shortest days of the year, and the longest nights. In the morning the blizzard raged harder than ever, with visibility down to a few feet. Our choices were gone; we had to get out, back across the pass to our sleeping bags, tents, food, and fuel. We started across the glacier, keeping within arm's length of each other to avoid becoming lost in the spinning snow.

The trail we had broken two days earlier had been erased by blowing snow, and we struggled to make a new one down into the glacier's bowl and back up the other side. We could not see through the blizzard the mountain skyline that marked the obvious gap of Bonney Pass, only a faint suggestion of three possible routes. Courtney and I debated which was the correct one. Three passes lead out of the bowl, each into different watersheds, and choosing the wrong one could be fatal. I thought back to the summer landscape, trying to remember the shape and details of terrain now buried.

The coach Bear Bryant once said, "If you make a mistake, make it at full speed." I picked what I believed to be the correct route, and we started up it because indecision wasn't an option. The daylight was fading, and it was pitch-black when we realized I had made the wrong choice. We started to dig snow caves into the side of the slope, desperate for some kind of shelter, but we hit rock two and a half feet down and the holes kept caving in. Finally we dug simple trenches, placed ropes and shovels in the bottom as insulation from the rock, laid ourselves down two to a hole, pulled our packs over the top of us, and Courtney buried us there. We could not turn over or move more than a few inches, and in the dark silence, they seemed more like snow graves than snow caves.

I might have begun to worry then. Our stove was out of fuel, and we were down to sucking chunks of ice for hydration. This was our third night out without sleeping bags. Our emergency food would be gone tomorrow. The blizzard showed no signs of giving up, and Courtney was out in it, marching stiffly back and forth in the cold and whirling snow, so someone might be there to dig us up in the morning, if there was anything left to dig. I might have been a little worried then, but because of Shackleton, and because of Mawson, I thought not about how bad it was, but how much worse it *could* be.

At least, I thought, lying in my snow grave through the long night. At least the ice beneath me wouldn't split in the night and dump me into cold ocean. At least I didn't have to eat boiled dog paws. At least I wasn't crawling a hundred miles on my hands and knees. At least the ship wouldn't leave without me while I watched it go. So I waited for morning, and it came with small puffing sounds around me. Courtney was out with the long, thin wand of an avalanche probe, systematically sticking it into the snow where he thought he might find bodies, all trace of last night's burial party erased. I could hear the probe sucking in and out of the snow, and then it poked me in the ribs.

I can't say that was the end of our epic, but I can say I lived to tell about it. We fought our way back to a camp that was obliterated under seven feet of new snow, and I won't tell about a certain scream-raising episode where I mistakenly added beef bouillon to the pot of sweet tea I handed up by a pole from the kitchen cave, now twelve feet under. But my point is the point from which we measure extremes. If your insight, whether gained from your own experience or garnered from someone else's, has been pushed to the frontier, you may be a long way off the ground, but you are not at the end of your rope.

That winter ascent of Gannett Peak pushed my margin of tolerance for snow and cold out to a point I have never again reached. Even at the time, I sensed it was a worthy investment into my future capacity. The experience has helped me during other difficult situations by giving me perspective, and it has helped my teammates. When they see me shrug at conditions they think are extreme, it pushes their own boundaries out to redefine the frontier. Any team, be it business or sport or academic, can benefit from this kind of insight gained at the margin, because it is a glimpse at how far you can really go. Someone on the team should always be out scouting the frontiers, pushing the boundaries, and coming back to adjust the team's scale and show the way to go on.

The important things you have gained from past experience can help you decide what to pursue in the future. It is that core sense of what you have valued that helps to clarify your direction and refine your compass setting. But don't forget that while you are a product of the mountains you have climbed in the past, and the mountains you are climbing now, most important you are a product of the mountains you dream about climbing in the future.

Aspiration is like a star shining over your Lifelong Ascent, pulling you upward like a beacon. It gives you a solid compass setting to move toward, a landmark in the distance to measure back from, a monument not to who you are, but to who you could someday be. We are better climbers today because our ultimate mountain is out there pulling us to try harder, learn more, and reach farther. A dream that is great beyond our abilities, a mountain that is harder than we imagine possible, can make us great in our aspiration to achieve it.

2. True success means more than standing on the summit.

> We climb the mountain not to stand on top, but to gain from the ascent. Choose your mountains according to what you desire to gain, and how that gain will contribute to your further ascent. True success is not defined simply by how far you go, but how much farther what you have gained will allow you to go.

"Everyone has an Everest inside," my uncle Courtney says. "It may not be a mountain peak, or a raging river, or a deep ocean, but we all have our ultimate challenges. It is reaching beyond our grasp, striving to go farther than we ever thought we could, that makes life worthwhile." Courtney's "Everest" really was Everest. That was his goal of a lifetime, and in 1988 he and my dad set off to climb it. My dad was fifty-eight, Courtney fifty-two, and between them and my older brother Orion, who joined the expedition, they had climbed the highest peaks in North America, South America, and Central America. On Everest, they chose the difficult Northeast Ridge route of Mallory and Irvine, crossing China and Tibet to get there.

They used no porters, deciding instead to give young American climbers a chance at Himalayan experience, even though all would have to haul loads, which made the ascent much more difficult. They wanted more than anything to *climb* the mountain, because that is what they had trained for, and that is what they dreamed about doing. They aspired to become the best mountain climbers they could be, and Everest represented the most challenging goal to move them toward that end.

Many difficulties conspired against them. They didn't have money or renown to ease their passage. They would receive no external rewards for success, and sacrificed much to make their dream a reality. Travel delays led to a late arrival at the base of

Everest, and sixty-two days later, after three summit attempts, tornado-force winds destroyed their upper camps, and descending winter weather forced them off the mountain without reaching the summit.* It became one of the greatest adventures in their lives, and the experience has enhanced their ability to meet other difficult challenges.

Were they successful? By the definition that equates success with standing on the summit, they were not. If that were the only criteria, they could have chosen an easier mountain, or an easier route up the mountain, or had Sherpas all but carry them to the top. But none of those options would have gained them what they were seeking, which was maximum improvement in their ability to climb.

When you are considering the question of direction and destination, understand that to gain true success, the expeditions you undertake should be chosen according to what you seek to gain, and what will move you further on your Lifelong Ascent toward your Ultimate Potential. Each goal is like a building block that raises the structure higher, and the more substantial and solid each block is, the higher you can build.

Still, there is a seemingly infinite number of expeditions and mountains to choose from, so how do you decide which of them to set forth on, and why? Your Compass, which is an essential tool to carry in the Personal Backpack you always travel with, can point you toward mountains that align themselves with the direction you want to go and can help you filter out those that don't. You should refer to your compass whenever you feel like you might be drifting off course, and if you are forced off course by obstacles in your path, you can use the compass to find your way back.

Your filter will naturally reduce the number of opportunities that fit on your compass-indicated line of ascent, but don't be content with those that are left. The mountains you see at the moment

---

*The "Cowboys on Everest" expedition was chronicled by Sue Cobb in *The Edge of Everest* (Stackpole, 1989).

are not all the mountains that are out there—you need to actively seek opportunities on the far horizon, not simply wait for opportunities to come to you. Once you have increased the number of potential mountains that match your line of ascent, you can analyze each to see which will take you farthest toward where you want to go.

Also understand that the "seemingly infinite number" of choices can be severely limited by outside forces, one of which is letting others define success for you. Success is often externally defined by traditional currencies: money, fame, prestige, applause. But these "hallmarks of success" are frequently by-products of true success, of doing something very well, and to pursue the reward while trying to bypass the solid foundation of enduring success often results in a bad ending, as illustrated by the number of bankrupt companies in the news.

If you allow your success to be defined solely by a consensus of merit, your choice of mountains will be limited to only those others recognize and find valuable. You will be the thousandth to be carried up the easy route on Everest, rather than the first to climb some unnamed spire in outer Mongolia that will truly further your Lifelong Ascent. You will be applauded more for climbing Everest, but applause can be one of the greatest saboteurs of aspiration. To gain applause, you only have to stand a little higher than your fellows. You are given a sense of arrival, bringing your climbing to a standstill, while your Lifelong Ascent is still asking for departures. And if all you seek is accolades, how will you go on if the applause dies down?

Our choices and aspirations can also be limited by resigning ourselves to a lack of opportunity. We might feel we've been funneled down a single track by circumstances and the walls are now too high to climb out, or we don't believe we can marshal the resources to change direction, or we don't ever seem to be in the right place at the right time, as if life were a lottery and success a matter of receiving the lucky number. But opportunity is not simply a matter of luck, good or bad. As the scientist Louis Pasteur noted, "In the field of observation, chance favors only the prepared mind." You might need to be in the right place at the right time, but if you are not standing at the threshold when the door opens, you cannot pass through. You can prepare for opportunity the way you prepare for any kind of expedition. If your climbing gear is packed, and you are constantly scanning the horizon for the kind of mountain you want to climb, you will be ready when opportunity knocks your door down.

Aspiration—who you want to become—is one of the greatest motivational forces you have to tap in to. You want to actively expand the pool of opportunities that reflect your aspiration, as well as consciously break down the barriers that conspire to limit those aspirations. You then have a choice of mountains that all move you in the direction of what you seek to gain, and you can select among them for which will move you furthest. When you begin that selection process, remember that success doesn't come from standing on the summit, but in rising to meet the summit, and if you choose an unchallenging summit, you will not rise far to reach it.

3. Choose the path of greatest gain.

> Goals with the most rewards are often the most difficult to achieve. We pick challenging mountains not because they are hard, but because we have the most to gain there. We are trying to become people with the ability to accomplish remarkable things, and for maximum gain we must seek ultimate mountains.

My sport is relatively simple: you start at the bottom of a cliff and try to get to the top. When I speak to business groups, I like to illustrate this point with a photograph of a canyon wall in Mexico where I have trained in the winter. It is columnar basalt, a volcanic rock that forms evenly angular corrugations, like a wide stairway tipped on its edge. Each section of rock looks just like the next, and this uniformity makes one "summit" indistinct from all the others. No point is really higher than the next, no cliff section obviously outstanding. But the difficulty of the climbing is not uniform, because minute variations in the rock make some routes easier and some more difficult.

I can drive to the top of this wall, and walk down a goat path to the base. I then have the choice of finding the hardest route up the wall, or an easier route, or I could walk back up the goat path. All end at the same place, which is not some inaccessible mountaintop. I could, in actuality, not even get out of the car, because I am on top already and could congratulate myself for being parked there.

But one of the motivating aspirations of my Lifelong Ascent is to be the best rock climber I can possibly be. My day's expedition to climb the wall, without reference to that aspiration, might be deemed successful if I chose either the easier route or the goat path, because I would have gotten to the top. But neither would make me a better climber, and, additionally, I would have lost the opportunity for gain toward my ultimate goal. If I simply stay in the car, not only will I not get better, I will grow worse. If any system isn't challenged, it doesn't stay the same—it atrophies. Every time I leave the ground, I am seeking nothing less than transformation, and the achievement of that goal most often lies on a path of great resistance.

Rock climbing, by any external definition, has no obvious practical value and might be considered foolish by some when risk is compared to gain. But what I value in climbing is that it asks for my best response on many fronts at once: physical strength, endurance, and flexibility; mental acuity in forethought, analysis, and problem solving; courage and tenacity of the spirit. I cannot gain an inch without applying these attributes, and I gain the most where the challenge is greatest.

When you are selecting your mountains, understand that you want to choose goals that not only move you in a direction you value, but move you maximally in that direction. With the choice of more or less challenging mountains, you must consider which will gain you the most success on your Lifelong Ascent.

We often base our choices on immediate gratification, what pleases or eases us at the moment. Without a more visionary framework to make choices, the moment is our only reference point. But those choices often affect us negatively in the future, sometimes catastrophically—businesses that collapse in the long term because they sought to inflate their stock prices in the short term, people who sacrifice their health in the end by choosing what made life more pleasant in the meantime. But even the threat of future consequences is not enough to change the way we make choices.

We need to move our reference point away from the moment and project it out toward our Ultimate Potential. When you make a choice, you don't want to ask, "Will the future catch up to me?" but "Can I catch up to the future?" The value of recognizing your Lifelong Ascent is that it makes you believe in the future—not a future of consequences, but a future of opportunity; not trying to avoid a negative, but to move toward a positive. When you envision who you could become, the light of that vision illuminates the path ahead and makes difficult choices easier because you can see where you could go.

To become remarkable people, we must see the extraordinary in ourselves and pursue the paths that lead us furthest toward our potential. Consistently striving to become more successful by choosing challenging mountains and climbing each to the summit leads to a Habit of Ascent. That is one in the list of essentials I have come to consider important to carry in your Personal Backpack. When ascent is a habit—a natural response to meeting challenge with an upward spirit—it is much easier to continue climbing. Obstacles are then mere detours, not dead ends; challenge is answered, not evaded.

I am grateful to my dad for teaching me a habit of ascent from the beginning, because habits learned early are the most enduring. While I spent the summers of my youth climbing and teaching survival, my winters were dedicated to skiing. My dad was an Olympic contender in downhill racing and became a ski instructor and racing coach so my older brother, younger sister, and I would have the same opportunity. He was insistent that every turn we made coming down the slope be a conscious attempt at improvement, and he stood there and watched, and analyzed, and demonstrated, and watched again, diligent and omnipresent, until the idea of continual improvement through disciplined practice became ingrained in all of us, and his actual presence was no longer needed.

And while the goal of the moment was to be better at each turn, the aspiration was the Olympic ideal of becoming best in the world, and it was from that summit back that we measured ourselves every day. When I went off to college, my passion turned from skiing to rock climbing, but what I gained from competitive skiing was a hunger for the pursuit of excellence, and the habit of striving to achieve success, which I could apply to any field of endeavor.

A habit of ascent is one of the keys to unlocking the door to opportunities. When you pursue rewarding mountains to their summits, each accomplishment becomes a foundation block that raises your belief in yourself. When you believe in your potential to become equal to a challenge, you expand the pool of options to choose from. You don't automatically say, "I can't do that because I've never done it," but instead "I've never done that but I *have* done all these other things, and success in one endeavor can be applied toward any endeavor." A habit of ascent also increases your skill, knowledge, and ability, which widens the playing field because you have more resources to pursue opportunities when they appear.

So when you ask which is the better path to take on this day, consider what you stand to gain from each alternative. To decide what you should do today, you must know where you want to go tomorrow, and where you would like to arrive a year from tomorrow. The step beyond where you are is fueled by the intent to take that step, and intent is generated by recognizing value in the ascent: reaching higher ground is always preceded by a passion for seeking higher ground.

4. First the dream.

Who you are is not nearly as important as who you aspire to become. It is critical for the dream to come first, before you are daunted by the analysis of what it will take to achieve your end, before you decide whether it can be done, because the dream itself has so much power to pull you beyond where you think you can go. Do not limit your future by basing it on the past, projecting what you *can* do based on what you *have done*. Your goal is to be not just better than you were, but as good as you can ultimately become.

If you were asked to project a challenging mountain on the line of your Lifelong Ascent, a mountain you had every reason to climb because you would gain from it things that you value, what would that mountain look like? How big would it be? How difficult and sustained the climbing? How long would you have it take to climb this mountain? A week? A year? Twenty years? Would you measure your endurance before you chose the size? Would you take into account your skill before you assigned the difficulty?

If you and I were like most people, we would add ourselves up to see what we were capable of, consider how much we were willing to commit, how many resources we had to contribute, design our mountain to accommodate those factors, then take off 5 percent to improve our chances of success. It might be an imposing mountain—lofty, admirable, even award-winning. It would certainly be climbable, because we envisioned it that way.

But if we placed our self-designed mountain next to a truly ultimate mountain, one we couldn't see the top of because it stretched into the clouds, one whose uncertainties could not be planned for, where the route was unknown and the rewards uncountable, the two would not be at all comparable. Instead of 5 percent below, our real ultimate mountain might be 500 percent beyond what we know we can do. Is it also climbable?

I ask the question to point to the difference between a goal and a dream. A dream is a mountain larger than we know we can climb. While goals are the mind's answer to destination, dreams answer to the heart, that belief that imagination can take us to wondrous places. Goals ask for action; dreams provide direction. Trango Tower was a dream for me, because I did not know if it could be climbed. That motivated me toward the goal of becoming good enough so I could climb it. A mountain half the size would make me only half the climber, for a dream that is close to your present capacity will not draw you nearly as far as one that has not been limited by what you know you can do.

As Thoreau pointed out, "If you have built castles in the air, your work need not be lost; that is where they should be. Now put foundations under them." Whenever you can, you should base your goals on dreams, because the feel of a goal tied to a dream is entirely different from a goal without a dream—you are pulled instead of pushed. A dream is the motivational force that makes your destination worth going to. Even if the goal at hand is not your actual dream, if it moves you toward a dream on the horizon beyond, it can share the same lift.

The factors that limit your aspirations can also limit your dreams. Your past can be a limiting factor if you allow it to be. The past can be a real danger to the expansiveness of dreams because we so often look at where we have come from before we allow ourselves to imagine where we might go: "That is what I have done, therefore this is what I can do." When we gauge our future potential based solely on past accomplishments, we always choose a mountain smaller than we could actually climb.

The weight of the past can sometimes pin us in place—it took so much to get this far on the ascent that we cannot imagine climbing higher. Past failures, past effort, setbacks, disappointments—when we can't leave that weight behind, it is too much to carry on. If the past weighs you down, empty it out of your backpack and make a fresh start. The reason that youth can dream so big is because it has so little past to hold it back.

In the present, a sense of arrival can limit dreaming. We win awards, and that suggests we must have accomplished all our dreams. We get rewards and assume we are already on top. Why go any higher when you are already a dizzying ways up? Because where you are is not where you can go.

I was asked by a very successful company to speak on this subject, because the CEO was concerned that his employees were too complacent. This company was the best in the world at what they did, and they had no close competition. Why, everybody asked, should they attempt to climb a bigger mountain, with all its risk and difficulty, when one the same size as last year's mountain was obviously climbable, and they would still be best in the world? "Why isn't a little better than others good enough?" they wanted to know. Better than others, I reminded them, is *not* as good as you can ultimately become. In freeing yourself from comparison with others, you are no longer tethered to their limits.

Even the future can put limits on dreaming when you don't believe in it—if you think the hand you've been dealt is the only one you have to play with, if you don't encourage yourself to reshuffle the deck, if you are convinced there isn't enough time left to win at the game. To continue to aspire you must find the direction that will gain you what you value, and dream about great mountains that could take you there. It doesn't matter whether others find value in your dream, or how many different dreams you pursue through life. But it is essential that the dream comes first, because it represents not what is likely, or even probable, but what might be possible.

5. Assume the sensational; pursue the impossible.

When a mountain is known to be climbable, the summit will be crowded and the route there overrun. To be a first ascensionist, you must think beyond known

summits. Because the unimaginable dreams of only last week become today's level of assumption, the platform of pursuit must be continually raised to leap beyond the present. If something is said to be impossible, that might be reason enough to try.

My mind-set for dreaming is to work continually on the frontier, to be a first ascensionist. If any piece of rock has been climbed anywhere, I have no drive to climb it myself because it has been shown to be achievable. If someone else has done it, I can eventually do it also, for the questions have already been answered. But on the frontier, the answers aren't known, and we often don't even know the questions. That is where the greatest gains are made, by launching into the unknown.

I didn't start on such a high ledge, but have reached this point by continually raising the platform of my pursuit. Aspiration has to be an evolution, because goals, once reached, must be recalibrated to continue your Lifelong Ascent. Aspiration often begins with admiration—wanting to emulate someone who is better than we are, and striving to become as good.

When I first started getting serious about rock climbing, at college in 1977, it was a sport still on the fringes, cultlike in its small circle of practitioners, infinite in its potential. There was no money attached, no structured hierarchy or referees. People pursued climbing as another skill of the outdoors, or simply because they loved to leave the ground, for there were no external rewards save a certain notoriety for seeming to taunt death from unhealthy elevations.

Because the sport was relatively new and formative, its leaders—those on the frontier of their time—were especially mythical, and the routes they put up on vertical stone were legends to be dreamed about, far too great for mere mortals. And in this arena I felt very much a mortal. At the University of Wyoming I was lucky to meet a fellow rock climber who was light-years ahead of me in knowledge and technique, for my skills were keyed to the 1950s era of my father's first ascents.

Paul Piana was from a small town in eastern Wyoming. I was from a small town in western Wyoming. The university was in another small town with a fine climbing area nearby of weirdly cracked and stacked bulging knobby granite. We were isolated from the larger climbing communities, places like Boulder, Colorado, and Yosemite in California, but we would read about what was happening there in the thin climbing magazines with their grainy, black-and-white photos.

And we were insulated from the rating system that was being defined on its upper edge by mythical climbers like John Gill, Jim Collins, John Bachar, and Tony Yaniro, a system that measures the difficulty of ascent from 1 to 5, with 1 representing a meadow walk, 3 approaching vertical, and 5 requiring technical skill and safety equipment. The fifth class is further divided into degrees of difficulty that increase with the decimal number. A forty-foot vertical ladder would fall just below the 5.0 rating because of the size and security of the hand- and footholds. Remove two-thirds of the rungs and that ladder might rate 5.5. The difficulty of a route is affected by the size of the holds, their distance apart, and the degree of slope. A rock-faced chimney would come in around 5.7 if the mortar was set back half an inch, but tilt that chimney out ten degrees and the difficulty could increase to 5.11. A brick wall with few gaps in the mortar, while merely straight up, might be a nearly impossible 5.14.

In 1960 the frontier of climbing was approaching 5.10 in difficulty. By the late seventies it had been pushed out to a seemingly mythical level of 5.12. There were no 5.12s in Wyoming when Paul and I started to climb together, and we had no idea how hard that really was. We would read about climbs like "Tales of Power" in Yosemite, or "Psycho Roof" outside of Boulder, and when we thought about them, we could hear harps, and angels singing. We would traverse the stone walls in our dorm's basement, back and forth, back and forth, and hang on fingerboards at night when we should have been studying, and do pull-ups on doorframes between classes, anything to increase our strength and power in an attempt to rise toward that extreme level.

In 1979 Paul and I finally took our first road trip to Yosemite, to see what we had been dreaming about. It was like going into a cathedral, shoes off and head down. Paul still laughs at my trepidation when I began leading "Tales of Power." I expected it to be so much harder, and I kept thinking I would come to the hard part and be stopped. We were both astonished when I completed the route. We had imagined it to be so impossibly difficult that we had trained correspondingly hard in preparation for what we had imagined, and we ended up much stronger than we had to be.

We were shocked by our success and realized that the routes we had been creating at our local area were as difficult as anything we knew about in the world at that time. It was exactly our isolation and insulation that had propelled us to the climbing frontier, because we had nothing to measure ourselves against but dreams and legends, and nobody to tell us that we couldn't climb something harder than had ever been done. We could be visionaries purely because where we were mattered not at all, but where we might go meant everything.

The real value of aspiring to what somebody else has done is that it begins the process of aspiration. Paul and I never dreamed we could go beyond the climbs we read about; we were only trying to approach becoming equal to them. The standard was set for us, and we rose to meet it. But where, then, when you have met your heroes, do you go next?

It makes me think of two brothers near Paul's hometown who climbed on boulders at their own local area. They were only interested in short, extremely gymnastic problems of movement, and they aspired to be like John Gill, a legendary boulderer whose book of outlandish climbing feats—captured in black-and-white photographs more powerful than video because they froze the improbable in midair—was read like a Bible, in short passages, because you simply couldn't consume it all at once.

These brothers were also isolated, working in their own small climbing area to somehow approach the feats of Gill. Not only were they insulated from the larger world, they started to insulate themselves from each other: one became this static power master, and the other a specialist in dynamic moves. Nobody could repeat their boulder problems, and they could not repeat each other's.

Like Paul and me, the two brothers eventually took a road trip to see what they had been dreaming about. When they succeeded on all of John Gill's boulder problems, they went home and eventually quit climbing. They had exceeded their aspirations, they had nothing more to pull them onward because suddenly they were out ahead, and they lacked a new destination to draw them farther. That is the danger in aspiring only to what someone else has already done, and why reevaluating your aspirations is essential to continued gain. Achieving your aspiration should give you courage to raise the platform to a new level, to set the standard higher even if you are out ahead. Remember that the magnetism of a mountain's pull is created by the magnitude of the dream. To accomplish great things, you must dream remarkable dreams.

If you aspire beyond what you know to be possible, how do you know if it is impossible, if you will be wasting your time chasing the end of the rainbow? In truth, the term "impossible" is applied more to things that have not been done than to things that cannot be done. Impossible is what you look for as a first ascensionist, because it clearly marks the frontier. Just setting your sights on it makes it merely improbable.

Pursuing the impossible is a creative way to expand your ability to both recognize and encounter opportunities. If your aspiration is not limited to what has already been done, your imagination is always looking for what hasn't been done. You cannot find what you do not seek, and the farsighted can always recognize more mountains on the horizon. The pathways to the impossible are rarely crowded, which leaves room for the intrepid to forge ahead. And the rewards of attempting the impossible, however you want to measure them, are the real opportunities of any unclimbed mountain.

In the 1980s Paul and I continued to find new heroes to admire, for European climbers swept in with breathtaking ability and raised the American standards by a full notch. When we reached that new platform, we again had to reevaluate, for what was above us now was untraveled ground. We were looking at the biggest walls in North America—multiday climbs up sheer faces thousands of feet high where you didn't come back to the ground until you had reached the top. The difficulties in all aspects were enormous.

We would have to become pioneers, because there were no guidebooks to show the way. We would have to be first, and it is so much harder to break trail than to follow. What makes it easier is belief in your ability to raise yourself. While aspiration begins with admiration, and adjusts itself to achievement, in the end the only thing your aspiration can be anchored to is the pursuit of your own Ultimate Potential. The more fantastic your aspirations, the farther you will go.

2. THE MIND BEHIND THE MOUNTAIN

Foundation Thinking
from the Top Down

California's Yosemite Valley is a cathedral of big walls, a climbers' Mecca stretching back more than half a century, and the scene of rock climbing's most spectacular advances. I was in the middle of a six-year pilgrimage to various hallowed climbing areas when I arrived at Yosemite in the spring of 1985 with great aspirations and little else. I was seeking new masters and realized the sole instructor who could teach me was the rock itself, and the only way to learn was to pass each vertical test before I moved on.

After finishing college, I had begun to travel from one climbing area to the next, and for six years the only roof over my head was a tent or the battered steel of my old VW van. My yearly income was gained from working two months each fall as an elk-hunting guide. Winters I would head south to Hueco Tanks outside of El Paso, Texas, where short, extreme boulders increased my level of pure gymnastic power. Summers would find me at Devil's Tower in northeastern Wyoming, where the dramatic volcanic column jutting from the plains offered perfect, six-hundred-foot thin cracks.

In between I traveled from the American Southeast, where the sandstone climbing was a delicate matter of wafer-thin edges, to the New York Shawangunks, where power ruled over finesse. From Mount Lemmon in Arizona to City of Rocks, Idaho; Colorado to Washington, Nevada to South Dakota. From technically extreme Smith Rocks in Oregon, to Joshua Tree in the southern California desert, where solo (without a rope) climbing meant your mind was your only safety net. If you made each move like you might die, you quickly would. Instead you had to move with serene fluidity, as if the ground did not exist. While climbing in rural Mexico, I was shot at, and in Egypt thrown in jail (they thought I was a spy). I unexpectedly won a bronze medal in a Russian speed climbing championship in Yalta, the rules of which were translated and shouted to me on the way up, and I bouldered on World War II–era concrete bunkers in Poland.

In the Western Europe of southern France and Germany, I learned the philosophy that had allowed Europeans to climb more difficult routes than Americans had achieved. In Eastern Europe's Czechoslovakia and East Germany, I saw the boldness that allowed them to climb more dangerous, poorly protected routes, and the siren's song of pursuing danger for the sake of danger, which became for many an end and the end. At every area, I arrived as the "visiting team" and I would automatically be taken to their most difficult route, where if I failed it would raise their own esteem. They were actually helping me by trying to hurt me, because I was seeking the most difficult tests where I could learn the most, and I couldn't have asked for better tour guides. But I was never content to repeat what had already been climbed, and looked through the guidebooks of every area for what hadn't been done.

My six-year road trip taught me to be comfortable with the unfamiliar, and to be willing to look for the answers wherever they could be found. I believed as a climber I would be better served to have a million impressions all different, than to have a million reinforcements of the same impression. And I knew there was an application out there for all of my acquisitions; I simply could not yet name what that application would be.

When I arrived in Yosemite in the spring of 1985, my first test was a beautiful hundred-foot thin crack called The Stigma. Almost all the difficult routes in Yosemite had been climbed first using "aid," a process that relies on slings and ladders to ascend, thus climbing your equipment instead of climbing the rock. I was only interested in using the natural features of the rock to gain ascent, a technique called "free climbing," which was an evolution of the sport made possible by increasing gymnastic application and ability in dedicated climbers who used ropes and equipment only to protect their falls.

Many of the aid routes were thought too difficult to free climb, including The Stigma, but after nine days of effort I succeeded on the hard 5.13 ascent. It made me think, *If this, then . . . ?* By far the most audacious challenge in the valley was an aid route up the sheer, immense southwest face of El Capitan named for climbing pioneer John Salathé. The Salathé Wall was considered by many to be the finest rock climb in the world. Several attempts had been made to free climb the Salathé, but it ultimately proved too much, and the prediction was that if it ever happened, it wouldn't be in that decade.

Paul and I had long marveled at the potential of the Salathé, inspired by previous attempts, but daunted by the magnitude. It was a mountain on the far horizon, glittering but inaccessible from where we thought we were. It was an ethereal dream and might easily have remained so. Opportunity, I will state again, is often a matter of both preparation and chance.

As its name suggests, El Capitan is the dominant feature coming in to the valley, rising precipitously to seventy-five hundred feet a quarter-mile from the main road. The sunny meadow at its base makes a pleasant arena for tourists and climbers to lie back and view the ascents in progress, and I was walking through that meadow one day when I saw a climber I knew looking through a telescope at the Salathé Wall. "Take a look," he said. I gazed at the granite features, legendary landmarks traced in stone—The Heart, a huge valentine-shaped depression a third of the way up, The Hollow Flake below The Ear leading to El Cap Spire, the overhanging Roof, Long Ledge, and finally the summit thirty-five hundred feet up.

My friend had heard about my free climb of The Stigma. "Todd," he said with conviction, "if you can do that, you can free the Salathé." He stated it with such a tone of assumption that I could not help but believe him, and in that instant the dream shifted from ethereal to merely improbable. Within three days I had put together a team to go up the Salathé to see if it might be possible. That reconnaissance wasn't exactly a disaster, but it was far from a masterful effort. I had no experience on big walls, didn't know how to haul equipment up with me, had spent a few nights on ledges but never had to live with the kind of exposure I was facing there. Still, I didn't see anything that looked like I couldn't climb it if I tried persistently enough, and with the summer heat rising, I drove back to my camp at Devil's Tower with an equally rising level of belief that the dream could come true.

I was back in Yosemite the following spring, testing the Salathé again, and improving my big wall skills. A difficult 5.13 climb thirty feet off the ground is technically no harder than one three thousand feet off the ground, but tell that to your pounding heart and sweaty palms. You may not believe this, but climbers are more respectful of heights than most people. The extreme height created other problems, because big wall climbing is like backpacking, only vertical. You have to bring your support system with you: sleeping bags, shelter, stove, fuel, food, water, and all the equipment for a safe ascent. The most efficient way to bring it up is in haul bags at the end of a rope passed over a pulley attached to a fixed point and tied to yourself at the other end. Step off the rock and you go down while the haul bag comes up, hopefully not at a high rate of speed.

To move up the rock using only the rock's natural features is to play a solitary game of Twister tipped on edge. Gymnastic free climbing is like solving puzzles of movement, and the harder the puzzle, the more attempts it takes to solve it. It is a ballet where you are both the choreographer and the dancer, determining the sequence of movement and rehearsing those sequences until they can be combined into a complete performance.

A long climb is divided into "pitches," limited by the length of the rope (usually 150 to 200 feet) and the nature of the rock that allows a secure belay point. Belaying is what keeps climbing safe because one person (on belay) is always in control of the rope to arrest a fall. That means only one person at a time can climb, and the leader must wedge pieces of gear into the rock (from tiny brass wedges to expanding cam devices to bolts placed in rock where there are no cracks) and clip his rope into the gear to avoid falling too far. The leader reaches a secured belay point at the end of the pitch, and the partner then climbs up removing the gear placed by the leader, to be used again higher up.

Before I began the Salathé, the longest climb I had done was around six pitches. The Salathé had thirty-six pitches. I focused more intently on the difficult rope lengths that spring of 1986, and again thought the whole could go free. But believing the wall could be climbed and actually climbing it were two very different things. I knew it would require unprecedented time living on the wall, for many of the hardest pitches were near the top. It would demand tenacity, even fanaticism. But it had become my shining star, the one light everything would be pointed toward, the impossible that could become possible if I tried hard enough to make it so.

When Paul and I motored in to Yosemite in the spring of 1988, we came prepared to lay siege. We started up to begin choreographing the hardest pitches and declared ourselves tenants of the wall, living on the rock for a week at a time, then coming down to resupply. The exposure was almost paralyzing, and our movements were choppy and panicked at first. Flow is critical in climbing, but to achieve good flow, you have to be relaxed. The only way to become relaxed in such an extreme environment is to spend time there, and it took a full three weeks of living on the wall to gain that sense of relaxation. In the meantime, I often had to purposely launch myself off the rock into a thirty-foot fall, over and over, to convince my mind that the consequences were not as extreme as they appeared, a process I called "getting velocitized."

Ultimately, the hardest part of big wall free climbing is not the exposure, but the acceptance that there is no instant gratification. A difficult short climb might take days of attempts to reach the top, but you get to sleep on solid ground at night, and the end is always in sight. We could have aid-climbed this wall in three days if our only goal was to stand on the summit. But to gain what we set out to gain, we had to accept our gratification in small parcels and take joy in the process. Our amusements were limited to twice-read books, tall tales, launching the occasional tortilla into a UFO orbit for observers below, and dreaming of where we could go from here.

After thirty days of testing solutions, we had only partially worked through all the puzzles of this wall. Then we reached another kind of crux. Between the two of us, we had $12.47 left to continue our quest. If we sold off our surplus gear, we could stay one more week, but to successfully climb the wall we still had to link the puzzles together from bottom to top in a command performance, climbing each pitch without falling. This was our last chance of the year to get it right.

We came down off the wall, sorted through our few inessential possessions, and held a yard sale at Camp IV, the infamous climbers' camp that provides Yosemite with much of its colorful reputation. We counted the proceeds and realized we didn't have enough money for tortillas, our wall staple, but we did have enough to buy flour, and I spent an industrious evening building tortillas with the durability of shoe leather, a product Paul fondly called "Manna from Hell." We had borrowed two hanging tents to sleep in on the wall—aluminum-framed nylon cots with a tent-like removable cover suspended by a single anchor strapped to the four corners. They were state-of-the-art at the time, but "stable" was not a word you could apply, as they had a bucking-bronc tendency to dump you off if you rode poorly in the saddle for even a moment.

The morning curtain opened on our command performance, and we started up boldly. The first ten pitches were less than vertical, glacier-polished slab climbing, ending at the base of the valentine Heart. A series of ledges led to the first more difficult pitch, a delicate traverse to Hollow Flake. The pitch up Hollow Flake couldn't be protected due to the gaping width of the crack, and we didn't realize our rope wasn't long enough to reach the next belay point. As I neared the end, Paul pulled his belay and "simul-climbed" with me, a potentially lethal action he neglected to tell me about at the time: "What you don't know can't kill you," he said with a shrug. We spent a quiet night on Hollow Flake Ledge, knowing that the worst was yet to come.

The next morning we shimmied up the inside of a chimneylike fissure, rounded the notoriously flaring Ear (which Paul deemed the scariest 5.7 in the world), and met up with our first 5.13, a vicious dihedral that used up the rest of our day and much of the skin on our fingers. We camped in The Alcove behind El Cap Spire—an eighty-foot detached column fifteen hundred feet off the ground and a familiar home during many of our earlier reconnaissances. Above the spire the route wandered from crack to ledge to face, and back to a crack streaming with water and slimed by moss, which Paul cheerily volunteered to lead with invectives still echoing among the crevices. We camped on the last semilevel perch of the car-hood-sized sloping Block.

The next day we were only able to work through three pitches before anchoring our hanging tents in the shelter below the great Roof—a two-story upside-down staircase three thousand feet off the ground. We would make this our home for the next three nights as we worked on the daunting overhanging headwall above us. Paul started out the next morning to tackle "The Great Barrier Roof," a scary proposition because it was not just up, it was up and out, like being suspended over the Grand Canyon. He swung from hold to hold like a gymnast on giant monkey bars, moving farther and farther out into space. I held my breath at every swing, hoping he would catch the next hold. If he missed, the fall would be spectacular. I breathed a final exhalation of relief when he got a fist jammed in the crack at the top of the Roof and pulled himself over the lip.

We worked on the 5.13 pitch above the Roof with only partial success, then rappelled back into the hanging tents that evening. As night descended, we could see far below a snaking ribbon of tiny headlights streaming into the valley. *It must be Friday,* we thought, the ritual weekend California rush away from the cities as distant and unreal as the pavement far below. The next day we finally succeeded on two of the three remaining 5.13 pitches and spent Saturday night hanging out three thousand feet up with a stone roof over our heads. We fought our way up the last difficult pitch the next morning, landing at Long Ledge. We hauled our camp and equipment up to the ledge, and with unsuppressible excitement decided there were enough hours left in the fading day to make a dash for the summit three pitches up.

We only took a moment at the summit to celebrate—wahooing, shaking each other's hand, and appreciating the view—then we had to rappel back down to our camp at Long Ledge, where we spent a joyous evening commemorating our victory and talking intensely about other walls that might now go free. Far below, a snaking ribbon of tiny headlights was streaming out of the valley. "Look," we said, "it must be Sunday." The next morning was a small matter of hauling all our gear up to the summit, then descending by the East Ledges—part scramble, part rappel—which was the traditional exit trail of climbers on El Cap.

Paul went up first, anchored the ropes to a big stone block at the top, and began hauling up bags. I followed the bags to help them along, using ascenders—devices that climb the rope by moving freely upward, but locking when pressure is applied downward, a process known as "jumaring." When I reached the top, Paul clipped my rope into a piton to the side as an extra measure of safety, then made me stop and model for a picture in the exact pose and place where climbing legend Layton Kor had stood twenty years earlier. "Give me a stalwart look," he said. "No, more winsome." I gave him the most stalwart, winsome look I could manage, and he tripped the shutter. It was the last photo that camera would ever take.

As I stepped up onto the rim and began to help Paul get the bags over the lip, we heard a terrible, deep cracking noise, and when we turned around we saw that the huge block everything was tied to was grinding slowly toward us and the edge. Paul put his hands against it, yelling, "No, no!," trying to stop the tons of moving granite. We had used the block as an anchor numerous times before, as had everyone for the past twenty years, and we could not fathom that it chose this unfortuitous moment to fracture on an invisible plane and begin to slide off its base. I tried to lunge out of the way, but a loop of slack rope had caught around my back and under the moving rock, and as the block ground closer, the rope tightened until I was pinned to the block and the last breath of air was squeezed out of me.

Right when I thought I would be cut in two, the moving block severed the rope with a loud crack like a rifle shot, and I was launched over the edge. In times of crisis, events often seem to slow down, and I felt like everything was happening underwater. It took five eternal seconds for that block to grind six feet to the edge, almost pause, then tip into a thirty-five-hundred-foot free fall to the talus below. Miraculously caught by one uncut rope, I dangled below the rim and watched the block slowly go over, just kissing my shoulder on the way down. I was hanging there unable to breathe, gasping for air and grasping for a solid hold on the rock. Paul said he heard a squeaky voice cry, "Grab the rope!," then saw a bloody hand reach up and snatch at the ascender, elongated and smashed onto the rope by the crushing block, the only thing that saved my rope from being cut and myself from joining the block's fatal descent.

Paul had also tried desperately to get out of the way of the moving block, but was caught in the same tangle of ropes and pinned as the block slid over his leg, crushing the bone in five places. He was dragged to the edge and fought his way back over ropes slithering beneath him like snakes as they were yanked off with the block. We lay at the top, shaken, unable as yet to consider ourselves fortunate, and wondered how long it would take rescuers to reach us. We were certain there would be a rescue because it was noon in the middle of high climbing season, and it must be obvious from the flying debris that some kind of accident had happened. We learned only later that people had reported seeing bodies fall off, and the rescue team was looking for us in the timber at the base.

It was cold at the summit, with patches of snow still lingering, and when we reached for our haul bags to put on coats to delay the onset of shock, we retrieved only cut ropes. It was all gone— matches, sleeping bags, jackets—everything that would allow us to survive the night there. Wearing only T-shirts, we realized we had to move if only to stay warm, so we started down the East Ledges, normally a two-hour descent, carrying our longest fragment of rope, and expecting to meet the rescue team coming up. Paul's leg looked hideously battered, with a deep hole in his ankle that didn't bleed because it had been cauterized by the pressure of the rock. I had two broken ribs and was coughing blood, and a muscle had been ripped from my hip with a piece of bone attached and I could not pick up my left leg, so we literally began to crawl off the mountain.

We would move a ways, then stop and listen for the rescue team. When we got cold, we moved again, never thinking we would have to get ourselves all the way down, never believing we *could* get ourselves all the way down. Five hours later we reached the first rappel point, and we both had a terrible time trying to get over the ledge using only one leg. It was getting dark when we finally reached the timber at the base, and I left Paul to crawl while I hobbled toward the main road, picking up my lame leg in a convulsive attempt at rapid locomotion.

I flagged down some climbers in a VW Bug who were reluctant to give me a ride until they saw Paul crawling out of the timber. They drove us to the park hospital, whose staff decided Paul needed surgery they couldn't provide, so the next day we literally hopped into Paul's decrepit VW van and drove back to Wyoming in a three-legged race, with Paul in the passenger seat running the shift, my one mobile arm steering, and my right foot running both the gas and clutch for my useless left leg. The starts were a bit rough, but once we got up to fourth gear, we really flew, if you could call fifty-three miles an hour downhill with a tail wind flying.

It took months for us to fully mend, but it was useful time to reflect on what we had gained. The first free ascent of the Salathé was hailed as a great breakthrough in the sport of rock climbing, and Paul and I were heartily congratulated. One of the points that interested me, though, was the availability of the opportunity. It wasn't like the wall had just been discovered, or the park had been closed to climbing and was suddenly open. It was not a new idea—others had contemplated it and even attempted it. It wasn't even a new level of technical climbing difficulty. And to those who value climbing, it was considered a true gem. Why, then, were we the ones to make it a reality?

What was new about the endeavor was the arena. We took a familiar game and moved it to a larger playing field, and this elevated contest was exponentially more complex and less certain of outcome. It was in essence new terrain, and the people willing to step across the frontier boundary are fewer than those who stay safely behind. I wondered why that is so, and the answer I arrived at is threefold. People don't cross the frontier boundary, one, because they see there might be risks there they can neither predict nor prevent; two, they don't recognize the value of the rewards to be gained there; and, three, there are too many questions that cannot be answered before they begin. Considering the forces that align to stop you, how can you cross the line and step boldly into new terrain?

6. When you journey off the map, how you think is more important than what you know.

In new terrain, there will always be more questions than answers, but you must not let a lack of illumination stop you from seeking further light. Even if you don't search out new terrain, you will find that the ground often shifts beneath your feet, and the maps of yesterday no longer apply. You cannot wait out on the plains for the answers of how to climb the mountain, but must go to the mountain to discover how to climb it.

The frontier is defined by unanswered questions, its shadowy boundary marked by a lack of illumination. What you don't know weighs more there than what you know, and when the scale is tipped toward uncertainty, that imbalance can make the boundary appear uncrossable. The American frontier of the nineteenth century was no Great Wall separating the civilized from the uncivilized, no chasm or moat to deter advances. It was a gradual dissolve from the known to the unknown. Some people crossed it and some did not, and if you could ask each who did cross why they went, what do you think they would say?

Some simply couldn't stop themselves, because they desired to know the unknown, to go and "see the elephant." The rest were seeking to improve their lives. Opportunities most often appear in new terrain, whether that terrain is new to you or new to the world. To go after those opportunities, you must cross the line of uncertainty, and the reluctance to take that step keeps many people from realizing their full potential. I see it in climbing all the time—a cliff on one side of a valley is crowded with climbers repeating well-known routes, while a cliff on the other side is empty because there is no guidebook. They have the skill to climb on the far cliff, the ability and the knowledge, but they wait for someone else to illuminate the way.

But why not stay in familiar terrain? It's comfortable there, and safe—and limiting. Repetition of the familiar is the antithesis of gain on your Lifelong Ascent. The very word "gain" implies a step beyond where you are, and that step often lands you in unfamiliar terrain. The curious thing about the frontier is that it actually moves with you. Each step forward extends the boundary of the map and redraws the known world. The opposite, unfortunately, is also true. Each backward step you take shrinks the map and diminishes the known world, and where you once went without trepidation is now filled with dark valleys and fearful outcomes. Clearly, the larger your map—the more places you go and challenges you are willing to meet—the more opportunities become available. And when opportunities do rise up in front of you, you don't want to be stopped by the uncertainty that comes with new terrain.

So how do you successfully cross the line of the frontier? First you must understand that on the frontier there will always be more questions than answers; uncertainty marks the boundary line. But the reason you go there is to find the answers. You must seek the solutions where they can be found, not expect them to arrive at your door. You would step forward confidently if you had all the answers before you began. But in new terrain the real key is to become confident in your ability to find the answers, and the best way to gain that confidence is to cross the line frequently—to seek out new terrain so you can learn how to cross it.

Second, you must be able to recognize the rewards to be found in the frontier. Sometimes they are the obvious traditional currency—money, prestige, advancement—but more often they are less obvious modes of gain—progress on your Lifelong Ascent, the excitement of discovery, satisfaction in accomplishment, new skills you can use to climb higher—that may or may not incidentally be accompanied by traditional currency. You should not use traditional currency as the sole determinant of potential reward, because it isn't the only currency out there, and many times the road to riches is constructed of stones others find valueless, carried back from far places and laid in line to get where you ultimately want to go.

Third is the issue of risk, which inevitably comes with new terrain. Imagine all the things that could go wrong. Imagine how you might respond. Identify what exactly you are risking. Resources? Your reputation? Your life? Are the risks greater than the rewards, and if they appear to be, can you adjust the formula to give yourself better odds? Consider what you are risking if you don't go. People are often stopped by the sensation of risk, warned away by an impression of danger without reasoning out what they are afraid of, and determining if it warrants fear or merely consideration.

On the Salathé, Paul and I could imagine nothing we had to

lose. Our most valuable resource, time, could not be better invested. We weren't concerned about our reputation because a reputation isn't worth having if it means standing still to defend it. We never believed we were risking our lives, because we had learned to pursue the sport safely. Barring a freak accident like a huge block falling unexpectedly off the rim, we figured we were in more danger of getting hit by a tour bus crossing the road to the base. There is a danger in trying to overinsulate yourself from risk to the point where you lose the reward. I've seen climbers so afraid of rock fall that they can't move with any efficiency because they are constantly dodging shadows. They proceed so cautiously and are on the wall so long that they do eventually get hit by a rock. "See!" they say, "I told you it was going to happen."

The ability to step into new terrain exists entirely in the way you think. A Frontier Mentality is one of the essentials to carry in your Personal Backpack. It is made up of four important qualities that you can cultivate in yourself and your organization. One is *an explorer's desire to discover the unknown.* All things extraordinary and remarkable are new things—new products, new paths, new ideas. It is much more exciting and energizing to lead the way than to follow, and to capitalize on that energy is to make much greater strides on your ascent.

Two is *a realist's understanding that you are the greatest variable.* Of all the factors in an equation that can be adjusted, *you* have the most potential for change. Rigidity is the enemy of ascent. To believe that you can't do something because you have never done it often means the end of the expedition, or you get left behind. If you think you are not good enough to climb that mountain, you're probably right. But that doesn't mean you can't become good enough.

Three, *a pioneer's willingness to improvise and adapt,* means setting forth without all the answers, while carrying the belief that you can find a way through. It isn't the memorization of details from past mountains that will help you on a new climb, but the way those mountains taught you to think. You gather what knowledge you can, but knowledge itself is no more animated than a book. It is using the knowledge that helps the ascent, and laying aside what doesn't, understanding that because something worked before doesn't mean it will work again, and, inversely, because something has never worked before doesn't mean it won't work now. Don't believe your opportunities are limited by what you know, or that you must be held back because of what you don't know.

And, last, *a dreamer's belief in shining mountains beyond the known horizon*. There are wonders and treasures out there to be found, and the people who don't believe that are the ones who stay home. The dream is what launches the expedition and fuels the search for answers. The more audacious the dream, the further it can take you. It is the recognition of potential reward, the pull of a lofty summit, the idea that the impossible could become possible that makes the journey worth the investment.

All of these qualities of a frontier mentality were tested on the Salathé climb, and the results gave me the courage to go on to other mountains. Of the numerous discoveries we made in this new terrain, one of the most valuable came not from reaching the summit, but from seeing the power that comes from setting out with the commitment to reach the summit. If our intentions had been tentative, "Let's go up one more time to see if it can be climbed," we would not have succeeded in climbing it. I also realize now that you cannot be anything but tentative if you set forth without a committed destination.

7. Define your mission.

The mission to climb the mountain must be described in photographic detail before the expedition is launched. Determining the parameters of your mountain allows you to plan toward what is actually real versus what you wish to be true. Answering where you are going provides a fixed summit to both move toward and measure back from. And understanding

why you are going there provides a reason to complete the climb.

The dream of the mountain is never quite the reality, because when we dream the sky is always blue, the rock is solid, and the natives are friendly. If you set out to climb the "dream mountain," you will likely be stopped by the first obstacle you did not imagine. The beginning step in defining your mission is to take a hard look at the true parameters of your mountain. What is the mountain made of? How will you get there? What kind of climbing skills will it ask for? How much support will you need? How long will it take? What is the climate like? Will there be others on the same mountain and how will they affect the outcome?

It is important to determine which of the parameters of your mountain are truly fixed, and which can be adjusted in your favor. My mountains can't be moved to a more convenient location; I can't change the elevation, or affect the weather. Those factors are unchangeable, and I must prepare accordingly. But I can adjust the season in which I go to climb the mountain, and that will affect the weather, making that seemingly fixed factor more of a variable. You don't want to assume that any parameter is fixed until you have imagined possible variations to adjust it in your favor.

Time is the parameter that climbers most often believe is a fixed limit on their mountain, whether it is the interval between plane tickets, or a calendar year. You don't want to determine the time frame first, then decide what kind of mountain you can climb in that interval. Time should be the last parameter to fit around the mountain. And even if the time frame is truly fixed, the use of that time is not. What you accomplish toward your goal in a day is in many ways more important than how many days you have to accomplish it.

Understanding the parameters of your mountain will help you immensely in the preparation stage of the expedition. If you can't envision what the climb will ask for, you can't imagine what to take with you. Solid planning requires a solid mountain. While the parameters can solidify the base and edges of your mountain, they won't necessarily define its summit, and a mountain without a summit is a climb without end. You must specify your summit point exactly before you ever leave level ground. This is a critical step of the expedition, because the summit is your defined destination and becomes the source and foundation for all your decisions. Only when you know where you are going can you actually arrive there.

I cannot emphasize enough how important it is to define your summit point before you begin climbing. In the equation of the climb, the summit is the fixed number on the right side of the equal sign, the answer that allows you to find the numbers on the left that add up correctly. If that answer is nebulous, every other step will be nebulous because you won't know what you are moving toward. And the climb must have a definitive end to generate the passion, commitment, and belief required to succeed on the mountain. Any climber will lose enthusiasm if the mountain has no end, which is why the summit point also needs to be reasonably proximate. If you have chosen a five-year mountain, you need to define summit waypoints on the route that can be marked, believed in, and celebrated within the larger ascent.

Given the importance of a concrete destination, why don't people always define their summits? One reason is that when you state a goal, you are expected to accomplish it. If you fail, there will be consequences, if only disappointment. It's less risky to just climb when the terrain is favorable and hole up if it starts to get difficult. You are still gaining altitude, but how much more could you gain if you had a destination and a plan to reach that destination? Committing to a summit might seem like a risk, but in fact you are risking more if you don't commit because you cannot ultimately climb as high.

At the other end of the spectrum are people so eager to begin climbing that they postpone defining their summit. I suspect that many small businesses fail for this reason. They see the direction they want to move, and they start climbing. Then the route forks.

Which way do you go? If you don't know your destination, it's impossible to discern how to get there. Then the climbing gets difficult. Is this as high as you ever intended to go? How high is high enough? Then the weather turns bad and you wonder why you ever began the climb. What was it you were trying to do? Without a shining summit point to pull you, you run out of reasons to go up.

The reason you are going up is the final leg of defining your mission. Once you have chosen a mountain and defined its summit, you need to review once more whether that mountain will actually advance you in the direction you value, and if the defined summit will move you maximally in that direction. We all have inspired ideas that, when penciled out, don't lead exactly to where we want to go. It is better to discover this discrepancy now, in the concept stage, than after you have launched the expedition and are halfway up the mountain.

This lesson was brought home to me when Paul and I set out to climb the next of what we had determined were the four greatest big walls in North America. Wyoming's Mount Hooker was a two-thousand-foot-high beauty in our own backyard, and we had dreamed about it before we even heard of the Salathé, but again it was an ethereal dream. After the Salathé it became a good application to test what we thought we had learned, with some new twists thrown in. The Salathé was within strolling distance of civilization, while Hooker was a hard twenty-five miles into the wilderness. Its elevation, just under thirteen thousand feet, would provide an element of altitude. Royal Robbins and team had impressively made the first aid ascent of the cold north face in 1964, and we wanted to accomplish the first free ascent.

Joining our team was renowned photographer and mountaineer Galen Rowell, and power man Tim Toula, known in climbing circles as TNT. With only a week to complete the expedition, we made short work of the wall, free climbing the route in three days. When I reflected on what we had gained there, I realized some of the mistakes to learn from were merely matters of comfort. We had brought no hanging tents, assuming there would be convenient ledges to camp on. The first night we were stranded by darkness, with each man seeking refuge where he could. Galen stuffed himself into a crevice, and Tim tried to balance on a ledge the size of a shoe box, buffeted by a bitterly cold wind. Paul and I passed him there while rappelling down to other bivouacs, and Paul described his expression in the headlamp as "reminiscent of a starving puppy who is made to sit in ice water while watching a Thanksgiving feast—truly, the most pathetic visage I've ever encountered."

The true mistake took a year to understand and involved the line of our ascent. We had picked a route that largely followed the initial aid ascent, but it was not the most rewarding route we could have chosen. The hardest pitch was 5.12, well within our ability. Still, we reached the summit we had chosen, and by that definition the expedition was a success, and we were congratulated for our accomplishment. But the climb had lacked the magnetic pull of the Salathé, as well as a deep feeling of accomplishment, and we didn't quite know why.

The following year we set out to climb the third on our list of North America's greatest walls. Mount Proboscis was seventy-five miles from a road, way up in Canada's Northwest Territories in the Cirque of the Unclimbables of the Logan Range. When Royal Robbins, Dick McCracken, Jim McCarthy, and Layton Kor went to aid-climb the South East Face in 1963, it was the most outrageous thing they could imagine, and it hasn't changed. Paul and I blocked out a month in the summer of 1992, piled into Galen Rowell's Suburban, and the three of us drove north for two-thousand-plus miles, caught a float plane, then a helicopter to land at the base absolutely speechless. The wall was two thousand feet high, and it was surrounded by cliffs of equal magnitude—a big wall paradise.

We immediately began to study our intended route following the 1963 aid ascent, but our eyes kept wandering two hundred yards left to a stunning arête going directly up the wall and forming a perfect corner, as if part of the wall had abruptly stepped back fifty feet. As a geological feature, it was amazing, but was it climbable? The whole of it was overhanging, leaning out eight feet from vertical, so something dropped would crash far out onto the talus below, and the rock looked glassy smooth. Galen saw us eyeing this outrageous feature and gently pointed out that since we had come this far, we might want to choose a route we knew could be climbed.

Aid routes almost always follow the great weakness in a wall, because that is where the ladders of ascent can most easily be placed. The Robbins route traced a crooked line of cracks up the wall. We looked at it, then back to the arête, and finally realized what we had done wrong on Hooker. We had let our line of ascent be defined for us by time constraints, historical values, and the guarantee of success. It ended up more of a feather in our caps than a foundation block beneath our feet. We have since come to believe that every wall has one truly great line, and the arête that Paul began to call "The Great Canadian Knife" was this wall's greatest line. To correct our thinking after Hooker, we immediately decided that since we had come this far, we had better choose a line that made the journey worth taking, and every other option disappeared.

The route proved absolutely beautiful, with tiny knobs and thin cracks and the corner of the arête itself providing pieces of the puzzle of ascent. There were enough 5.13s to test our ability, and enough uncertainty to test our resolve. We might never find another big wall that was so much fun. When we finally reached the summit, we had a true feeling of accomplishment and knew that we had gained a greater capacity to go on to higher mountains.

When you reach a summit defined for maximum success, you have then gained all that the mountain has to give you. The summit represents the accomplishment of your goal, which is why the summit point has significance. But remember not to mistake the summit for the goal. You can take a helicopter to the summit, but your goal is to climb the mountain because of what you have to gain in the ascent. That is also why you never want to summit "at all costs," a caution many mountaineers fatally forget in their altitude-induced fog. The reason you are going to the summit is to gain the ability to keep climbing, to further your success, and decisions that get you to the summit without regard to the reason you are going there can harm your ability to go on.

It brings to mind the example of a company I spoke to celebrating their champion salesman. I saw him get an award for climbing the highest mountain that company had ever seen, with summit sales figures that were unbelievable. I found out later that the salesman had promised extraordinary things that the product couldn't deliver. Because his field was a matter of life and death, his buyers were outraged, and not only did they not want to hear from him again, they didn't want to hear from the company again—ever. The salesman ended his own ability to keep climbing, and he severely limited the company's.

Clearly, all the salesman thought about was reaching an extraordinary summit, not how to reach that summit in a way that would allow him to go on to an even loftier one. You must always look beyond the summit for the reason you are climbing the mountain. Because the summit marks the end of what you have to gain on that mountain, once you have reached the summit, it becomes the least important point on your ascent. But because of where it will lead you, the summit is always the most important point during the climb. Your destination provides the answer for every step, and to successfully climb the mountain, you must keep that destination always in view.

8. If you leave the summit point out of your equation, you are guaranteed to drift.

Once you have defined your summit, you are not just going up, you are going up with a destination, and all your decisions must be based on arriving there, not just moving upward. When you know where the last step will end, the biggest step has already been taken.

> At every step you must continue to ask yourself not
> "Will this get me higher?" but "Will this get me to
> where I'm going?"

All the steps we take on a mountain are taken toward the summit.
Our allegiance is to completing the journey, not just gaining
height. This may seem obvious, because the goal is to climb the
mountain, but we are so conditioned to being congratulated for
getting higher that we often don't consider if that rise is moving us
toward our destination. We look instead to the accumulated past
and applaud ourselves on gaining a little ground from there. And
when we are consistently celebrated for rising, we will do about
anything to keep rising. But to get to the summit, we might need
to down-climb or traverse to avoid a section of blank rock that
could end the climb.

The tendency to climb without regard to the destination is most
marked when the summit is poorly defined: "I want to be better"
versus "I want to arrive at this point." Clearly defining your summit gives you a solid destination, but you still have to ask yourself
if you are moving toward it, or simply moving away from where
you were. Many climbers hold tenaciously to a direction, but often
at the cost of the destination.

Once you understand the importance of basing all decisions on
arriving at the summit, you can begin to work out the mechanics
of movement. For some people this is the most complicated part of
climbing, because given all the options and considering all the details involved, how do you determine what the next step should be?
What must be done first? If you don't do this today, what will be
the consequences tomorrow, or a month from today? The steps up
the mountain are never an obvious staircase, and the combinations
and permutations are so numerous, and the consequences of a misstep so amplified, that you can be at a minimum uncertain, and
possibly paralyzed.

But I like to point out that movement is *merely* mechanics, and
"the next step" can be reduced to a logical formula. If Point A is
where you begin, and Point B is the summit, you solve for B by de-

termining the missing factors between B and A. Faced with a choice of options, the question isn't "Will this move me away from A?" but "Will this move me toward B?" Summit-back thinking is much more effective on a mountain than ground-up thinking. You always want to make your decisions based on what is most likely to land you at the summit, not launch you from the ground.

To simplify the complex equation of the whole mountain, you can divide it into manageable segments, and the summit of each segment becomes Point B. While you can only climb one rope length at a time, every rope length must still be considered in the context of the higher mountain. If you move in a way today that harms your ability on the final rope length, you may not reach the summit. If you make decisions based on what you want at the moment, you often fail in the long term. Look to the summit as the final arbiter when you don't know what answer is the right answer.

The mechanics of movement involve not just getting yourself to the summit, but stretching the support system that allows you to reach the summit. How do you get where you are going with what you have to work with? On an expedition, resources (including time and morale) often give out before the climbers do. You might attribute that to poor planning before you leave level ground, but remember that your planning is always based on more questions than answers, and in the field you have the ability to adjust the plan to match the mountain.

9. Always measure your progress and your resources from the summit instead of the base.

> You arrive at the base of a mountain with a stock of resources, many of which are fixed. You must allocate those resources according to what is ahead, always referencing how to get where you're going with what you have. The success of a day's action must be measured in meters from the destination, not miles from where you began.

As I stated before, summit-back thinking is fundamental to success on a mountain, and it involves not just how to take the next step, but how to support that step in a way that will allow you to continue to the summit. The resources that accompany your goal must go the distance along with the climber, and to accomplish that, all factors must be measured against not how far you have come, but how far you still have to go.

Take, for example, the resource of time. When deadlines are imminent, it is natural to think from the summit back, because the equation is ominously short between what you have to do versus where you must arrive. When the deadline is somewhere in the distant future, the tendency is to look to the past for your sense of progress, to gaze back at the end of the day at how far you have come since the morning. That thinking continues until the deadline is again imminent, and suddenly your resources are strained or fail before you reach the summit.

Measuring your progress from the summit back requires disciplined accounting. The farther you are from your destination, the more complex the equation of what remains to be done. A daily inventory that lists everything remaining on the left side of the equal sign will help you arrive at the right side of the equal sign.

A constant awareness of what remains to be done adds a critical boost to your equation by infusing the climb with a sense of urgency. We always try harder when we feel that urgency, we apply ourselves more diligently, we are more keenly aware that our performance counts. The last three-point shot in the basketball game is thrown with more concentration than the first, but in reality it might be the first that wins, or loses, the game.

It isn't simply a matter of making your resources stretch, but having the right resources where and when they are needed. A rope at Base Camp is a resource listed on the inventory, but that won't help if you are two thousand feet up and the rope is not. On big walls I have found that the formula must be delicately balanced. Because all your supplies must be hauled up with you, you don't want to bring more than you need because that uses up your strength. You can't bring much less than you need because that endangers your health. You must match the resources to the terrain with strategic balance. The best way to achieve that balance is to preclimb the terrain in your mind, to anticipate what will be needed before it is needed. To be able to anticipate the terrain, you must look up at where you are going, not down toward where you have come from.

You cannot climb the highest summits without mastering the mechanics of movement, but I want to point out that you also can't climb them without the motivation to move. The greatest way to generate motivation is in your choice of mountains, by having a summit worth reaching. Maintaining motivation is then a matter of review, reminding yourself what you have come to climb, and why you are climbing it.

In the mechanics of motivation, if Point A is where you begin, and Point B is your destination, there is a Point C beyond the summit, which is the reason you are going to B. It answers the question "Why am I climbing?" Point C might be this mountain's summit if you are struggling with a rope length, or the next mountain you are climbing toward if the whole of this one seems overwhelming, or a far point on the line moving toward your Ultimate Potential if you need something grander to imagine. Name it and place it wherever it gives the maximum motivation to pull you from A and through B. Make Point C the shining star that gives the ascent a magical light.

10. Carry a photo of the mountain as seen from the plains.

The photo represents the mission to climb the mountain. This is what you have come to do, and why you have come to do it. Whenever you lose perspective, and a small obstacle seems huge, whenever you want to quit, whenever you forget what you came for, the photo will remind you.

There will be many times on an expedition when you need to regenerate your motivation. If you have defined your mission in photographic detail, then you have a photo of the mountain to carry with you on the ascent. The photo of the mountain shows the mission as you conceived it, brilliantly lit, beautiful in proportion, hovering on the horizon like a castle in the air. It is a picture of the whole, not just the symmetry of the mountain, but the essence of the dream.

The photo of the mountain does not disclose the details of the day. It may reveal its perfect line, but it cannot tell you where to place your hands and feet, only why you are climbing. When the details of the day seem overwhelming, pull out the photo to expand your perspective.

When the mountain up close is too large to believe in, the photo can help you step back and gain belief. When a storm erases all the world outside your tent, the photo can remind you where you are going. When you are closing on the summit but your resources seem too scant to finish the climb, the photo can show you what a small distance remains.

The photo can illuminate both perspective and scalability. A seven-foot blank wall directly in front of you blocks both your view of what is beyond, and your confidence in your ability to go on. But in the photo that obstacle is diminished, and you can see there might be a way to get beyond it, and a value in finding the way. In the larger perspective, each mountain can be placed on the scale of your Lifelong Ascent where it is merely a step. That makes a challenging mountain less overwhelming because you can see beyond its summit. The most difficult mountains are those we can't seem to see beyond, but we often can't see because we don't look.

When Paul and I were living on the Salathé Wall and began to talk about other big walls it might be possible to climb, that gave us an application for the exacting lessons we were learning and added value to our effort because we were looking beyond where we were to see what we were moving toward. The last on our list of the four greatest big walls in North America would be the most daunting challenge we had ever faced, and we needed to expand our perspective to make that challenge approachable.

Yosemite's Half Dome is exactly what its name suggests, a giant mound of stone sliced in two like a round of cheese and eaten clean to the middle by erosion. The twenty-four-hundred-foot northwest face had a perfect direct line leading up to the overhanging visor of rock at its summit, and that line was the challenge we set for ourselves in the spring of 1993. We began with our usual enthusiasm and found the first two pitches were classic Yosemite crack climbing. But then we came to a seemingly blank wall of rock. For twenty frustrating days we tried to find a way up or around this impossible pitch, which Paul described as "climbing a color change." When we finally worked out a potential choreography, it was still discouragingly clear that it would take many days of rehearsal to put the movements flawlessly together, and there remained four more 5.13-grade pitches to work out.

I should have suspected from Paul's increasing and uncharacteristic glumness that he was losing his commitment to the siege, but I was stunned when he told me he was done. The next day he was leaving—we could pull the ropes and go back to Wyoming together, or he would leave me his gear and I could stay and find another partner. I didn't sleep that night, trying to decide how important this goal was to me, trying to convince myself that I could come back another year. But the only quality that had consistently paid off on the other walls was a bulldog tenacity. I believed that this wall could be climbed, and the only way to fulfill that belief was to stay and climb it.

I made the long hike down to Paul's car at Camp IV the next day to collect my spare clothes and odds and ends, which I stuffed into a paper bag. It started to rain as he drove away, and as I stood there watching, the bag grew soggy, then transparent, and then disintegrated. A team is not an aggregate of individuals, but an alignment of individuals who all believe the challenge is on the line of their true ascent, and I was now a team of one. I could not replace Paul as a partner to my dream, but neither could I climb the wall alone. I also could not leave. Only this mountain could make me good enough to climb it, and if I turned away I would not become the person I aspired to be.

The next morning I paged through the list of climbers I knew, trying to find someone who would join me. Nancy Feagin, a superb climber from Jackson, Wyoming, said she would come to Yosemite, but she only had twenty days to spare. Together we worked out another of the hard pitches and several of the more moderate ones, then her tenure ran out. If she had been able to stay, I know we could have succeeded. But she had committed months earlier to another expedition, and I watched in dismay as she also left.

I next convinced two talented technical climbers who were in Yosemite that they should join me, and with their backing finally conquered that first blank section of color change, a 5.13d I named "The Sleepwalker." But a difference of philosophy ultimately split us apart, and I was again solitary in my quest. I had now spent fifty days trying to solve this puzzle, set back by every partner change. I realized how important it is to have teammates who believe in the value of the goal, how they can reflect your own belief and amplify it. And I saw how critical it is to be able to see beyond the summit, to know what you are moving toward, and why.

Trango Tower was the next mountain on the horizon, my looming Point C, and if I could succeed on Half Dome, the most technically difficult wall in the world, I would have a better chance to succeed on Trango, the most difficult high-altitude wall in the world. I didn't know anyone else whose dream it was to free climb Half Dome, but I finally realized I knew someone whose dream it was to become a good-enough climber to attempt a mountain like Half Dome. Steve Bechtel was working in an outdoor shop in Casper, Wyoming, and I called him there to see if he might be interested in joining me. He quit his job on the spot and started packing.

Steve Bechtel was known in climbing circles as "the Chosen One," because from the moment he first showed an interest in the sport he had been carefully mentored by my friend Steve Petro—an incredibly strong and talented climber who developed many of the routes in central Wyoming's spectacular Fremont Canyon. Not many people could hold up under Petro's serious intensity, but Bechtel's talent had thrived along with his enthusiasm.

My next recruit was Chris Oates, a Canadian who was climbing for the summer at my home base in Lander, Wyoming. Each had a positive attitude and an extensive sense of humor, and they made an entertaining pair. They arrived at Half Dome with the commitment to stay till the snow drove us out, moving in like this was their new hometown, and hanging out address cards. The cardboard placard at one tent site read "Little Calcutta," the other was labeled "Copacabana" for its extra fifteen minutes of daily sunlight. They did not see this adventure as paying the price of opportunity, but as gladly investing in their future opportunities.

With their commitment and positive attitude, combined with all my earlier work, we finished the wall in ten days and drove happily back to Wyoming. The tenacity that had been asked of me on this mountain was extended past all previous experience, like the winter climb of Gannett Peak had extended my experience with snow and cold, and both would be seriously tested again on my next mountain. When I think back on it, the hardest part of Half Dome turned out to be not the difficult climbing, but maintaining my belief without a mirror to show me what belief looks like. The photo of the mountain reflects the dream, but the dreamer must climb the mountain to reflect what he saw in the photo.

3. LAUNCHING THE EXPEDITION

How to Choose a Team and Prepare for the Unknown

What I remember most about that fortuitous meeting with Voytek Kurtyka was the wild look in his eyes. Paul and I had just described our Salathé climb at the American Alpine Club's annual meeting and received the Underhill Award for climbing achievement. In the crowd that surrounded us afterward, Voytek elbowed his way through, took hold of my arm, and said, "I have something to show you." The wiry, high-voltage Polish climber had recently completed a difficult new aid route up the east face of Trango Tower in the Karakoram Himalayas. I had met Voytek earlier that fall at a conference in Canada, and I liked him immediately, but my image of Himalayan climbing was very much like everybody's—labored wallowing up long snow ridges under miserable conditions, with a focus on reaching the summit by any means possible. Even the easiest Himalayan route is arduous and worthy of admiration for the effort involved, but that kind of climbing was not at all in line with the direction of my own ascent.

So I was skeptical that Voytek could show me anything in the Himalayas to pique my interest. Still, I had recognized in him a kindred spirit. We shared a camaraderie in pursuit of the improbable, and I admired the extremity of his exploits. In his thickly accented English, he told us he was impressed by our willingness to fall, which I thought odd until I realized he meant we were willing to repeatedly throw ourselves at something that was beyond us at the moment, that falling wasn't the end of the effort but part of perfecting the effort. So we made room and time to look at his photos of Trango Tower, and what we saw was a revelation. Removed from the Himalayan backdrop, the rock might have been plucked out of the best of Yosemite's big walls. Beautiful sunlit granite, laser cracks, extreme vertical exposure. I had gotten used to thinking of myself as a rock gymnast, with no apparent business in the Himalayas, but I could see myself in his photos. At that moment it looked to me like I could pursue the same sport in the wildest arena on earth. "You should go to free climb it," he said, with an air that such a thing was perfectly reasonable.

In retrospect, I wonder that I didn't take a harder look at his assumption. What he considered reasonable was unimaginable to most people. He had come out of the forge of hardship that hammered behind the Iron Curtain. Restricted by travel limitations, lack of resources, and limited opportunities, for Eastern Bloc climbers it wasn't a matter of who had the desire to go on mountaineering expeditions, but who had the desire to find a way to go. Voytek had raised money by smuggling what was rare into the Eastern Bloc, and what was common out. Because of the travel restrictions, he smuggled himself as well. He described to me one long transaction that involved smuggling chewing gum into Russia, vodka out, two trips into West Germany, with the final product a single jewel equivalent in value to a new Mercedes-Benz. He sold the jewel for hard currency and smuggled that and himself back into Poland to fund an expedition to the Himalayas.

It wasn't just the intrigue of making things happen in a place where things weren't supposed to happen. The Eastern Bloc climbers were famous for facing down adversity, for going up in a storm when other, better-supported teams were retreating down. They made first ascents in winter, outrageously difficult climbs, because the peak fees were cheaper then. The hard routes that no one else wanted fell to them, and they often succeeded against all odds because they believed it might be their only chance. There was no guarantee that they could try again next year. The black-haired, hawk-faced Voytek talked about Himalayan storms the way most people mention traffic in their morning commute, a slowdown but nothing to be concerned about.

I have since come to realize that if someone tells you something is impossible, you should question the source of their belief. And if someone tells you, "Of course, it is possible," you should also question the source of their belief. But at the time I didn't know any better, and I placed Trango Tower on the far horizon. It was a mountain that would make all the other mountains look reasonable in comparison and would provide an application for everything I was learning in the meantime. As I completed each of the four greatest walls in North America, my level of belief rose until the idea of Trango began to seem plausible. It might be impossible, but it was certainly worth trying. In a way, Trango was my "last next." I could imagine nothing beyond it, and in that sense it occupied my whole horizon.

The problems seemed enormous. Trango might have fit well in Yosemite, but it was not in Yosemite. It was half a world away in the most hostile terrain I could imagine. The approach was long and arduous. The base of the tower was 17,500 feet high, and the summit crossed into the altitude death zone. We didn't know if climbing for hours with bare hands was possible in that extreme environment, or if storms would ice over the rock for so many days that we would lose the opportunity to climb it.

But the most daunting problem was Trango's hybrid nature. If you plotted the mountain on a graph where technical free climbing formed one axis, and Himalayan peak climbing formed the other, Trango fell in the middle. It was neither just one or the other, but both, and that middle ground might have been on the moon considering the scarcity of people who had ventured there.

This point was made clear to me when I set out to solve my most immediate problem, securing funding for the expedition. I approached several organizations that made a business of supporting the improbable. They consulted their experts, who declared the endeavor impossible and thus unfundable. Our chance of success, they said, was zero. I had a contract at the time with Reebok for sponsorship, and they ultimately came through with the $40,000 to fund the trip—a drop in the bucket for them, and an ocean of opportunity for me.

I now had money to get there, but I still needed a team to go with me. Paul broke his other leg in 1994, which unfortunately took him out of the picture. So with businesslike logic, I started looking at résumés. What I needed was someone with Himalayan experience, so it wouldn't be unfamiliar ground to everyone on the team. The only way to be comfortable in a Himalayan environment is to spend a lot of time in the Himalayas. I approached a Himalayan veteran with an impressive résumé, told him what I was going to climb, and he told me I was flat-out crazy. Something that technically difficult could not be climbed in that environment. End of discussion. I cast my net wider, inviting a British Himalayan veteran with an impressive résumé. No, he said, you have to be able to sprint between storms. That kind of climbing is too slow. It can't be done. I couldn't counter their arguments because I didn't know if it could be done. On the other hand, I had no real proof that it couldn't be done.

I then pursued the other axis, seeking out technical rock climbers with impressive résumés. When I showed them a picture of Trango, they might have believed they could climb each rope length if it was in Yosemite, but they could not see beyond the fact that this mountain would test more than their climbing ability. With a vision of storms and ragged breathing and weeks of unpleasant living conditions, they politely declined. I was beginning to see a pattern here, and it was formed by the things a résumé won't tell you.

11. The mountain doesn't give a damn about your résumé.

A climber's potential for success can be enhanced by the mountains they have climbed in the past, because it teaches them how to think about all mountains. But a summit list shouldn't be the primary qualifier. You are looking for people to do a job, not to have done a job, so the application must have room for aspiration, belief, and desire—what will be on their résumé someday.

What I began to realize is that if you depend on résumés to make your selection, you have to be aware of the limited information résumés provide. Number one, no matter how impressive the résumé is, the mountain will remain unimpressed. It cannot be climbed by standing on past accomplishment, no matter how heroic that accomplishment was. Movement beyond what has been done requires an upward step, and that step must be taken with the intention to take another, and another. Because you are looking for someone to do a job, not to have done a job, a summit list will never reveal the willingness to take another step.

A résumé also won't tell you how much an applicant desires to climb this particular mountain. You want the fire and enthusiasm that comes with hunger, a fanatical commitment to the goal, a core belief in its value. The technical climbers I tried to recruit did not see how the value in Trango could be worth the costs. They had zero desire. Even if I had paid them to come, they would never have given the magnitude of commitment and effort required to reach the summit. Money, after all, has only limited value. It is both a carrot and a stick, and each fails when the hill gets too steep.

Third, a résumé doesn't say how much weight a climber is already carrying in his backpack. The fatigue of mountains climbed in the past can weigh heavily on any mountaineer if they are unable to empty their packs of all that is nonessential to go on to the next mountain. The memory of past effort, the strain of unsorted responsibilities, the confusion of excessive details, all must be left behind when you are starting a new mountain. Remember, it is not the minutiae of your mountains you want to carry forward, but the way those mountains taught you to think.

But fatigue is not the only weight. The Himalayan veterans I approached were weighed down by preconceived beliefs of what was possible. Experience can teach you what is possible, but it can also make you think that a step beyond what you know is impossible. If you are the greatest expert in the world, who could better know the difference? But experience often looks to the past for answers to the future, and the future often asks questions that the past cannot answer.

Reputation can also be a weight that brings any ascent to a halt. What if you fail? Of all the things people are unwilling to risk, reputation seems to me the most expendable. If you must defend a position, you cannot climb higher. And if you don't keep climbing, you lose the ability to climb. In either case, others will eventually overrun your position and gain higher ground. If you allow yourself to be wrong, to fail, to take a step even if it is a misstep, it is easier to take the next step.

When I was contemplating my prospective team (or lack thereof), I began to wonder what would have happened if I had assembled a team before I had chosen a mountain, if I said, "Let's get two of the most experienced technical rock climbers and two of the greatest Himalayan veterans together on a team and see where we can go." On paper that team would appear capable of climbing a mountain like Trango Tower. But in the field, between the disbelief of one group, and the aversion of the other, we could only have climbed a moderate slope on the fringes of the Himalayas. Clearly I was thinking in the wrong direction. I had been looking for the best-qualified team, not the team best for this particular mountain.

12. *Without hunger, both skill and experience will remain in base camp.*

When you are looking for a team that can reach the summit, put forth a picture of your mountain and let climbers break your door down to join the ascent. You are looking not only for the tenacity and fortitude to stay, but the inability to imagine leaving. A shared sense of mission, with desire leading all other attributes, is a formula forged for success.

The people who ultimately made up the team to climb Trango Tower turned out to be the opposite of what I had initially been looking for. Their résumés wouldn't have filled half a page. They were all (with the exception of one) excellent rock climbers, but there are hundreds of good climbers out there, so basic skill wasn't an issue. When I had failed to find team members who could believe in this climb, I realized I had to look for ones who at least didn't disbelieve. Steve Bechtel, who had shown his ability to commit at the end of the Half Dome climb, seemed a natural choice. Bright and witty with an intellectual flare, the twenty-four-year-old from Casper, Wyoming, was an ideal companion and more important, he wanted very badly to go.

With Steve on board, Bobby Model and Mike Lilygren started knocking our door down. Although I didn't know them well, and they didn't know each other, they both knew Steve, and his enthusiasm for the project fired their own imaginations until they couldn't imagine being left behind. Bobby, a budding photographer as well as talented climber, had a reputation for being unkillable. The twenty-two-year-old Cody, Wyoming, native had recently graduated from the University of Wyoming and was primed for adventure. His gangly length and elfish features belied his deliberate nature. I found out he was steady, and he was unstoppable. Bobby would become the most fearless member of our expedition, to the point where we all had to be afraid for him, and he would take one of the most courageous steps on the climb.

Mike Lilygren had a schoolboy face and Dennis-the-Menace hair, an irritatingly endless sense of humor, and a tinkerer's mind for detail. The twenty-six-year-old was also a graduate of the University of Wyoming and had been a climbing partner with Steve on several wild adventures. He would turn into "the closer" on the expedition, the one who kept getting stronger as the burden increased, the keystone that bridged the way to the summit.

Almost as a side note, we included Jeff Bechtel, Steve's little brother, to come along as Base Camp manager. The twenty-one-year-old hunting guide and roustabout had no climbing experience, but he was strong and good-natured. Jeff would be the wild card on the expedition. We thought he came completely unprepared for this kind of challenge, but he carried in his backpack everything he would need.

On paper we did not look like the team to climb this mountain. None of us had been to the Himalayas, I was the only one with much big wall experience, and when we were met in Islamabad by the veteran Pakistani climber we had hired to smooth our way with the government, the first thing he asked me was: "Did you bring lots of milk?" I looked at him, astonished. "What for?" I asked. He pointed to my young, inexperienced team and said, "For the babies." But all of the things we didn't have would be balanced by what we did have, and foremost was desire.

It is only in retrospect that I can list the qualities I look for in a team, after trial and error, seeing what has worked and what hasn't, and the first on that list is desire. All the team members have to want badly to climb this mountain, because their degree of effort and commitment, their vision and belief, their ability to reach beyond themselves, all are correspondent to the degree that they value this climb. No other incentive will carry a team as far. You want them to be pulled, not pushed, and the only way to generate that magnetism is for each to see a tremendous value in reaching the summit. Quality of effort means everything, which is why I think it is critical for the mountain to choose the team.

When the mountain comes first and the team knocks the door down to climb it, you know they have the desire to go all the way to the summit.

Second on my list is a Unified Sense of Mission, and it is so important I consider it an essential to carry in the Expedition Backpack. A unified sense of mission begins with agreement on the summit, the destination you are going to. Everyone on the team must agree on the summit point, because it is the only fixed answer in the equation of the climb. While you are all moving toward the summit, you are not necessarily marching together in formation, so everyone must know what they are working toward and where they are trying to arrive.

Because you won't all share the same origins, background, training, or experience, and in fact you might never work together again, the only thing you necessarily have in common is this one goal, and that is the glue that bonds the team together. Care taken now to ensure agreement will not just solve problems later, it might eliminate problems from happening. If you don't all agree on the summit, you should never leave the ground. It is better to be shorthanded and unified than strong in numbers and weak in focus.

The other element of a unified sense of mission is commitment to the goal. If you start with highly motivated members who all see value in reaching the summit, you are halfway there. But the team also needs to be invested in the goal, and this is critically important. All the team members must feel like they are collaborators in regard to the dream. The more input and contribution they have into every stage of the goal's realization, the more stake they feel they have in the outcome, and the harder they will try to make that outcome successful. I made sure the team was involved from the beginning of the planning stage, and we each had input into making decisions that would affect the outcome. This was not *my* expedition, but *our* expedition, and that early and constant investment of everyone in the goal would pay off spectacularly for us all.

Third on the list of qualities I look for is the potential of a person to enhance the team's chance of success, but skill and experience aren't always the defining factors of that potential. A mountain asks for many attributes, and I look for qualities that make bridges as well as fill gaps. There is always at least one "and" in the qualifications: a good crack climber *and* good camping skills, logistics expertise *and* a sense of humor. I don't need everyone to be good at everything, nor do I want everyone good at only one and the same thing.

Because what I do is very difficult in many ways, one of the most important qualities I look for is a combination of tenacity and fortitude and durability and resilience, more briefly defined as toughness. You can't find a guy much more tough than a Wyoming cowboy. They eat sagebrush for breakfast, spit nails, and consider cactus a pretty good pillow at night. I had stacked my team completely with Wyoming cowboys, and although I could not predict what they were truly capable of, I hoped they would form an arch that grew stronger as the pressure increased. They were at this point 100 percent potential, and it remained to be seen what they could become.

Lastly, I look for team members who are willing to begin without all the answers. A lot of people want to go on adventures, start their own business, do something risky. What stops them? Opportunity, like an open door, has a threshold, and the willingness to cross that threshold is a quality that a person may or may not demonstrate. As Bilbo Baggins pointed out in *The Hobbit*, the hardest step is the one away from your front door. There is a terrible sticking point between desire, and action upon that desire—between wanting to take the step, and actually taking it. But if you invest the team in the entire process, the line between inaction and action becomes much less defined, and much easier to cross.

You might point out that this team joined me because they didn't know any better, because they were at a point in their lives where anything seemed possible. I didn't sugar-coat the difficulties we were going to face, but instead of turning them back, it only strengthened their resolve. I told them without question this mountain would be the hardest thing ever tried in the Himalayas, and they said, "Why not start at the top?" If it had been a lesser mountain, would their commitment and resolve have been proportionately less?

13. There is nothing more dangerous than a moderate mountain.

While an easy mountain often consumes the same time and resources as a difficult mountain, it can be more dangerous because you face the same objective hazards while your attention isn't focused because it doesn't have to be. Your team must be riveted to a mountain audacious enough to make them climb beyond themselves, and to cooperate so all will arrive together. On an ultimate mountain, there is no room for dysfunction, or anything but extraordinary and heroic behavior.

It often takes the same amount of resources to climb an easy mountain as it does a hard mountain. You still face the same dangers of exposure, rock fall, avalanche. You are still leaving level ground, with all the risks inherent in a climb. And for all that you have to lose on an easy mountain, you have less to gain: less reward, less improvement, less capacity to climb higher.

When choosing your mountain and defining its summit, remember to make your decisions based not on what the team *can* do, but on what the team *could* do. If you choose a lower summit to guarantee success, you might be creating a formula for failure. No one gives their best effort if they aren't asked for it. Teams don't work well together if it isn't required by the goal. The truth is, heroic behavior only appears under extreme conditions.

On a summit that is obviously climbable, you're likely to trudge along, oblivious to danger because you don't expect it. You can bicker with your teammates, do sloppy work, wander in your attention, waste time and resources, and, ironically, still reach that summit. You are a success by the definition of your goal, but by any other definition?

That same dysfunctional behavior can lead to failure on a mountain picked exactly to guarantee success. When a varsity team loses to the junior varsity, they have experienced "moderate mountain syndrome." Every other factor would predict their success: experience, talent, resources. But they did not view the challenge as worthy of their best effort. They are stunned at the result and ask themselves, "How could we possibly lose when it was so easy to win?" Of course they lost exactly because they assumed they couldn't lose.

Flip this example around to the junior varsity point of view. Here was something they shouldn't be able to do. To win, they had to play better than they had ever played in their lives. They had to support each other as a team, as well as excel individually. The very odds against their success was the genesis of the transformation that led to their success, and they will carry that win with them into the future, pulling out the photo to remember what an audacious dream feels like when you make it come true.

Moderate mountains are dangerous not only to the success of the Expedition, but also to the Lifelong Ascent, because they subvert you from real opportunities for gain. Not only are you missing the chance to climb a greater mountain in the same time frame, you aren't gaining the skills to climb the even greater mountains beyond.

Jim Collins pointed out in his seminal book *Built to Last* that the companies that succeeded most in the long run were not the ones which picked goals guaranteed to succeed, but those that risked the impossible summits. "BHAG (Big Hairy Audacious Goal)" is now a byword in the business world, but it is still a concept underapplied. You don't always have to pick a summit beyond anything done in the world, but you do have to pick one beyond anything done by your team if you expect them to transcend their past performances.

Remember that the more audacious the summit you choose, the more chance you have to achieve real success, because challenge is one of the greatest motivators you can find. A summit higher than you know you can climb increases both your desire, and your potential for reward. Your attention and focus will then be riveted to the goal, and because so many things *could* stop you, you are always looking for a way past what *might* stop you.

If you choose an easy mountain because you believe you can reach the top, instead of lowering the mountain, why not raise your level of belief? If you are afraid that your team isn't equal to the mountain, let the mountain make the team equal.

14. Only an ultimate mountain can forge an ultimate team.

As a team, we have the choice of parity—being equal to the sum of our parts; synergy—being more than the sum of our parts; or alchemy—becoming fundamentally transformed. The mountain is the catalyst that can change synergy to alchemy. This massive, ultimate goal creates a magnetic force that aligns and focuses the group into a team. It is only in answer to the mountain that the team transcends itself to reach the greatest heights.

Heroes are often ordinary people who find themselves in an extraordinary circumstance. They usually look into the camera with a bewildered expression and say, "I only did what was needed," as if we all might have done the same thing in their place. We often don't root for the best in a contest, but for who has come the farthest, who traveled the hardest road to arrive at this far place. We marvel at the human capacity to overcome adversity, not realizing that it is the adversity that makes us strong enough to overcome it.

When the underdog team unexpectedly wins the championship, it was the goal that transformed them, a reason compelling enough to reach beyond themselves, and to reach together in a solidarity of many minds with one vision. While they all must work together,

I want to point out that there is an "I" in ultimate team; a heroic team is made up of heroic individuals who understand that helping the team helps themselves.

It is only when we are asked for greatness by a goal worth reaching that we become great. All manner of exhortation to try harder, to be "team players," to support each other will be ineffective without a compelling reason why. You can threaten to bench them, or throw them off the team, but remember that you can never push someone as far as they can be pulled. The goal creates its own magnetism, and the more audacious the goal, the greater the attraction.

If your team doesn't appear extraordinary on paper, that is the last reason to choose a smaller mountain within their known ability. The mountain is the catalyst that can make them extraordinary. I might have had the least-qualified team ever to enter the Himalayas, but I had the most audacious mountain. And the members had signed on not to see if the mountain could be climbed, but to climb it. It was a goal worthy of their best effort, with a pull that would carry them way beyond who they thought they were, and toward what they could become.

To gain belief in the mountain they are going to climb, it is important to give a team enough lead time. When I have looked at expeditions where the team turned back short of the summit while all other factors said they could go on, I find that often that mountain hasn't been their dream for long enough, or never was. Belief is an infusion of the spirit. We may immediately see the possibility and recognize the value, but the belief in our ability and the commitment to reach the summit are often gained in increments. That is why, in this fast-paced world, the dream generator behind the team must be visionary—to look beyond the foothills in the foreground and see shining peaks on the horizon, impossible today, improbable in the near future, and remarkable in the end.

To eventually make the dream a reality, you must move toward the summit even when you are still out on the plains. The approach to the mountain's base is a minefield of questions that must be answered before you begin climbing. How do we get there?

What should we carry with us? What will the mountain ask of us, and how will we respond? Because you are crossing into the frontier, no one else can answer the questions for you.

15. The only guidebook to your mountain is the one you will write.

How do you climb a mountain that has never been climbed? There is nobody you can ask, no footsteps to follow, no manual with diagrams, so you must learn to write your own. Preparation for a new climb has to be a projection of what is correct, since not only do you not know all the answers, you often don't know all the questions. Plan according to what is known, add to that for what might be unknown, and be willing to fill in the blanks as you go along.

An expedition begins before you ever leave home. When any decision you make has the potential to affect the outcome of the climb, the expedition has already begun. So the time spent in preparation for the climb will be as important as your actual ability to climb and is, in fact, part of the climb. I emphasize this point because impatience, the eagerness to begin climbing, often propels people halfway up the mountain without the necessities to go on to the top.

The main question in preparing for the unknown is: "What are we going to need?" The first item on the list is information. You need to gather and analyze all available data about the place you are going to. Information cannot answer all of your questions, because you are crossing the line of the frontier, but it can point out potential hazards, fill in some of the missing details, and suggest lines of approach. It is important to analyze the information not just to establish its usefulness, but to question the source for validity and currency.

The information we could gather on Trango Tower was

excessively short on details. We knew the approximate elevation, finding at least three different figures that averaged 20,500 feet. We knew that its location was close enough to K2, the second-highest peak in the world, to have an established, though primitive, transportation system to get us there. We knew the weather conditions were good enough at times to allow free climbing, because the area is a desert largely unaffected by the summer monsoons so devastating on Everest, eight hundred miles to the southeast. And we knew that altitude would make the climb more difficult. Humans don't belong in such rarefied air, and each day stolen in the heights must be paid back at lower ground to recover from the ordeal. "Carry high, sleep low" was the first commandment in the Himalayan bible.

The second item on the list of what you are going to need is a support system, which falls under the expeditionary term of "logistics." How many ropes, how much food and fuel, what kind of travel connections, how will the supply line work, what are the options for resupply? How long is this expedition going to take? Some questions are harder to answer than others. Our estimate for the expedition was sixty days—ten days to get in and out, five to acclimate at Base Camp, another ten to establish interim camps up the wall, fifteen days to climb the two-thousand-foot main wall, and a twenty-day window for the contingencies of recovery, weather, and other uncertainties. We planned to rotate two teams up and down from Base Camp, to follow the Himalayan commandment to spend as much time as possible at a lower altitude, and we packed accordingly, weighting our supplies heavily toward Base Camp to burn kerosene and eat slow-cooking food like lentils and rice, while preserving our hotter-burning white gas and quick-cooking freeze-dried food for the short push on the upper wall.

I have found that logistics is both a science and an art. It is science in pursuing the question out to its logical end. How much rice do we need to pack? Take the amount of rice one person consumes in one meal, multiply that by the number of meals you plan to eat rice, times the number of people, and that equals the amount of rice you need to pack. The total rice I came up with by this formula was close to one hundred pounds. You look at a hundred pounds of rice, which is equal in size to a large trash can, and think, *My God, we couldn't possibly eat that much, let alone carry it. Let's take half the amount, which looks more reasonable.* Without the formula to support your decisions, it is pure guesswork, with consequences that could end the expedition.

People who aren't good at logistics often simply lack the perseverance to follow the question through to its logical end. But logistics is also an art, because not all of the numbers in a formula can be fixed. If you were following someone else's guidebook, they could tell you exactly what would be needed as long as you stayed on the familiar path. When you make your own path, you must extrapolate what you know and imagine what you don't know. The answers are a projection of what you believe to be true. You realize that for want of one quart of fuel, the climb could be stopped. With two hundred gallons too much, you might not make it to the mountain for the burden of carrying it. Overpacking can be as dangerous as underpacking. Logic will supply you with the minimum, imagination can provide a little extra for insurance, but the end goal is not to be right, because given all the variables you can't know if you are right. You simply want to be right enough.

When you have answered as much as possible "What are we going to need?," the next step is the acquisition of the elements you do need. The obvious elements involve your support system. We had to order tents far enough in advance to have time to apply waterproofing. The ropes had to arrive before we would depart. Nylon slings and aluminum carabiners, camp stoves and nesting pots, ascenders and descenders, shoes for rock and boots for ice, parkas and sleeping bags, solar chargers and extra batteries, water bottles and filters, peanut butter and macaroni, freeze-dried Stroganoff and powdered cheese began to pile up in my garage in Lander, Wyoming, and was divided as finely as mist into duffels, so if one bag was lost we wouldn't lose all of one critical element. When we completed the acquisition of our material elements, the whole weighed a colossal four thousand pounds. There might have been an ounce or two that was frivolous (we packed a freeze-dried beer-making kit), but none of it was random.

Material elements aren't the only elements you need to acquire to improve your chances of success at this stage. You also need to acquire more ability and belief. Any shortfalls you have at this point in strength or training will often be magnified on the mountain. Our biggest shortfall was experience in the Himalayas that would give us a degree of comfort when we arrived there. Himalayan convention said that to succeed at altitude you should train at altitude in the snow and cold, and we were advised to go there and climb a lesser wall to become acclimated to the conditions. The veterans just shook their heads when we trained instead on boulders in the Texas desert, where it was hot, dry, and low to the ground.

But it was a question of what was really needed versus what had ever been needed before. If convention could climb this mountain, it would have. You become acclimated to altitude only when you are at altitude, and once you come down, your body readjusts itself. To succeed at gymnastic rock climbing, you need muscular power, and altitude is devastating to muscle because the body can't synthesize ingested protein as well and begins to consume the protein stored in its own muscles. We understood that we needed to go in with as much pure muscle power as we could, or we would fail from attrition.

My winter training camp at Hueco Tanks, Texas, was the perfect laboratory for the acquisition of power, and the team gathered there for months of intense gymnastic skill and strength building. We picked the most improbable short stretches of rock we could find and tried to move across them, believing that if we could climb this ten feet, we could climb any ten feet. Boulders, after all, can be stacked into mountains. That kind of intense focus on the elements of your game not only raises your ability, it raises your belief in your ability. Belief is an essential when you step into the unknown—not belief that you know the way, but belief that you are prepared to find a way.

The year we spent training and preparing together gave the

Trango team belief not only in ourselves, but in each other, generating trust that would be critical later when the decision of one would affect all and there was no opportunity for consultation. It helped solidify agreement on where we were going and why it was important to get there. There is a tendency to focus on the material needs of an expedition while ignoring the mental requirements of the team—their concerns, their doubts, all the factors that isolate them from the dream and from each other. A cast of strangers goes to climb a mountain, and we wonder why, when the chips are down, it becomes every man for himself.

A business team is rarely going to have the same opportunities for team building as a sport team living together, traveling together, generating consensus and trust. An audacious goal can help bring a team together, but you still need to address the mental barriers that force them apart. Ask: What is the scariest aspect of this mountain? Which rope length appears most impossible? Where do you think things are most likely to go wrong? The psychology of success is about looking into your backpacks to see what is and isn't there, not simply starting up regardless of what you really need.

I want to stress that it is important to develop a plan, to answer the questions of what you expect you'll need for the expedition because it adds significantly to your chances of success. (When polar explorer Ernest Shackleton claimed he could launch an expedition on the back of a napkin, it was only because in his mind he carried all the essentials he would need.) And you make your plan based on what you know, projecting your best guess forward toward what you don't know.

We had come up with what we believed was a good, solid plan, based on logic, artistic interpretation, and the knowledge we had to work with. We could not foresee how very, very far the planned mountain was from the real mountain we found. In the preparation stage, and throughout the expedition, you must understand that only the mountain is written in stone, and plans are constantly subject to revision in answer to the mountain.

16. The best plan is the one that works.

Ernest Hemingway once wrote, "What is true at first light is a lie by noon." A plan can't be held to as dogma, because it was created according to what you imagined to be true, or even what was true yesterday, not what is actually true at the moment. You must be instantly willing to modify or even abandon your original strategy whenever the situation demands it. Ultimately, the only way to finally answer all the questions is to go to the mountain itself.

The phrase "It all went according to plan" implies that when we create a plan we always expect a perfect trip; we presume that reality will match our expectations. And sometimes the more minutely we plan, the more dismayed we are when things don't go according to plan. That is why it is important during the planning stage to understand that you are projecting your best guess, that the answers you come up with won't necessarily be the final answer. To hold to the plan instead of the summit as your reference point can make you fail to climb the mountain. So you not only have to be willing to deviate from the plan, or throw it out completely if the reality is the opposite of your expectations, you have to be willing to do it instantly, without consternation, without trying to force your footsteps back onto the prescribed path.

One way to reduce the disparity between expectation and reality, and build flexibility into your original plan, is to generate "what-if" scenarios. What if a bag gets lost in transport, what if the approach takes six days instead of three, what if a stove breaks down or a tent pole snaps? To anticipate where things could go wrong in critical places, and to devise strategies for correction, can help avoid a crisis when things do go wrong. There is a danger, of course, in trying to overinsulate yourself from exposure, in packing your bags for every conceivable occasion until you can't lift your luggage. The "what-if" game plan is more about how you think than what you carry for insurance. If you have anticipated danger, you can often see it coming and steer around it.

The importance of "what-if" scenarios was taught to me by Rick Ridgeway, who invited Paul Piana and me to join an expedition in 1992 to climb a twenty-five-hundred-foot granite "shark fin" slicing ominously out of the Amazon jungle on the border of Venezuela and Brazil. ESPN was sponsoring the endeavor through its *Expedition Earth* series, sending a film crew along to document the adventure, but Ridgeway was the real draw. One of this country's greatest adventurers, Rick Ridgeway was among the first Americans to reach the summit of K2, and a long list of other amazing accomplishments gave him a reputation that was by itself enough to convince us to join the expedition.

I was given the job of food logistics, with the parameters that we would travel up the Orinoco River headwaters for four days by dugout canoe, then hike for three days through some of the most remote jungle on earth to reach this fantastic mountain named Aratitiyope. I had only a week to pull the plan together, because I had just returned from a climbing reconnaissance in Thailand, and I was scheduled to go to South Africa in two months. I sketched out a menu for eight of us plus five Indian guides who would also act as porters, and we took off for Venezuela.

When we got to our departure point, we realized the logistics did not add up. Between the food, climbing gear, and camera equipment, we needed more Indians to act as porters, but the more numbers we added to the crew, the more supplies we needed to bring along to support them, and the more people we needed to transport the extra supplies. The spiral seemed unending, and it was about to swamp the whole effort.

"Why not," I asked, with a brilliant flash of inspiration, "parachute-drop two loads of supplies to the base of the mountain? Wouldn't that solve all our problems?" There was a consensus of nodding heads, and we started making arrangements for a plane. All along, Ridgeway had been asking, "What if this happens? What if that happens?," presenting these wild (and I thought unlikely) situations where certain plans went wrong. "What if," he asked as we were sorting loads for the plane, "we can't find the parachutes once they've dropped into the jungle?" To appease his paranoia, Paul and I dug out a minimum of climbing gear from the whole we had committed to the drop. We went up with the plane to scope the wall and mark in our minds the drop site as the parachutes floated down, then landed again and started up the river in the dugout canoes. Our final numbers had been increased from thirteen to twenty-two, including two Yanomami natives, each wearing only a red loincloth and equipped solely with a bow and a quiver of arrows.

The Yanomamis came in very handy as the four-day river trip turned to eight days of lugging up uncertain tributaries overswept with vines and fallen trees, when to preserve our precious food supply we had to forage in the river for piranhas, crocodiles, and eighty-pound catfish. When the boats could go no farther, we set off overland, hacking a way through the dense undergrowth and horrified that everything around us was either sharp, had a painful bite, or was deadly. I got a scorpion sting on my finger that swelled up and took three months to heal. It was dangerous to even sit down, and we slept in hammocks suspended between trees and draped with a bug net.

To find our way in the dense cover, we had to climb the tallest of the trees to sight the mountain and get a daily compass setting. On the seventh day of our "three-day" trek in, we finally reached the mountain and set out to find the parachutes. But we had not taken into account the three-layer canopy of the rain forest, and while the drop site was obvious from the air where the chutes had caught in the top canopy, the boxes could not easily be spotted looking up through the layers of vegetation, and we were eventually forced to give up the search. Another "what-if" scenario had come to pass. Contrary to being upset by these constant setbacks,

Ridgeway seemed almost pleased by our growing tribulations. The harder it got, the more he reveled in the difficulty.

I can't begin to describe the rest of the epic, but Paul and I climbed the mountain, getting by with short rations and the minimum of climbing gear we had kept with us, forced to suck bug-filled water from the bayonet-cluster bromeliads growing out of the rock wall. I might say that the moral of the story was this: when venturing into deepest Amazonia where there is nothing to eat but monkeys, it is good to have straight-arrow shooting Yanomamis always by your side. But what I remember most is how Rick Ridgeway, who had seemed so overcautious about what might go wrong at the beginning, had a determined, hunkering grin and a glint in his eye when things did go wrong, and the tougher it got at the end, the bigger his grin.

The final danger in the preparation process of an expedition is the tendency to postpone leaving until every question has been answered, forgetting that the mountain is the only place the answers can definitively be found. In the meantime, you can be buried under a mountain of excess preparedness before you ever step out your door. No matter how well prepared you are, how honed your climbing skills, how vast your expertise, you cannot climb the mountain if you don't get to it. So at a set point, you must quit preparing and actually begin.

We had the benefit of a climbing season to define our window of opportunity, and a plane ticket to mark our departure date, but many expeditions can be postponed endlessly because we don't believe we are quite well enough prepared—there is still a question unanswered, an uncertainty that does not guarantee the outcome. It is important to set a departure date, not only because then you will go, but because then you will have a deadline, a Point B to work back from. That sense of urgency allows you to set priorities and accomplish intermediate goals.

The night before we left for Pakistan, we had a party in Lander and I swear half the town showed up. Our well-wishers were setting off industrial fireworks in the street, and toasting us from kegs of beer, and I wondered about Heinrich Harrer's observation that "it is a bad thing when the band plays before you set off for the mountain." When the last reveler staggered home that dark night at the end of June, I felt like I had just cut loose a balloon, and where the wind would blow it I did not know.

4. FACING THE WALL

Making the Critical Transition from Horizontal to Vertical

Islamabad, the capital of Pakistan, is a planned, modern city of wide boulevards and soulless architecture, a façade laid out on the broad plain at the feet of the ancient city of Rawalpindi, with its narrow alleys spilling with bazaars, where the smell of spice and the sound of wild music rises amid the jostling crowds. We arrived at the airport in Islamabad in the middle of the night with our mountain of baggage and eluded a request for a bribe from the customs official by telling him to go ahead and search every one of our bags. We had all night, we said, and he waved us through with disgust.

But our problems with the government were just beginning. Bill Hatcher, the photographer who had come along to document the expedition—a climber I'd known since college and shared many adventures with—had added an assistant at the last minute, Donna Raupp, who would also be our medical officer. We had faxed ahead her visa application, but it had not yet been approved, as the wheels of government turned exceedingly slowly here. For seven days we were trapped in the sweltering 127-degree heat of Islamabad, making forays into Rawalpindi to shop for what we hadn't brought with us, and fighting to keep momentum against the grinding inertia of the unplanned delay.

With the visa finally in hand, we piled our two tons of gear into and on top of a bus more highly decorated than an Oriental rug and squeezed ourselves in, as well as our liaison officer (a colonel in the Pakistani army, and a required member of the expedition). Our driver, a fierce-looking tribesman whom Jeff nicknamed "Wild-eyed Charlie," got us out of Islamabad and on the road toward the Indus River. Several hours later we came to a fork in the road, where a turn to the left would lead to the infamous Khyber Pass into Afghanistan. We could never go that way, the liaison officer told us. Because we don't have enough fuel? Because we don't have the right visas? "No," he said matter-of-factly. "We don't have enough firepower to fight our way through."

The right fork followed the Indus River gorge to the city of Skardu, a twenty-four-straight-hour trip with the bus stopping only for meals and to switch drivers. As the gorge narrowed, so did the road, forming a single lane gouged from the steep hillside of raw and tumbling earth. We began to see the wreckage of trucks and buses by the river far below, some still burning, and people standing on the edge of the road staring down with stricken looks on their faces. Wild-eyed Charlie would blast his horn at every blind curve, and again when he met another vehicle in a game of chicken, where metal nearly scraped metal squeezing past each other and only barely slowing down. Through it all, Charlie never changed expression. To show fear was to concede the game. My respect for Himalayan climbers went up several notches on that bus ride—we could easily have died right there, and some had.

We eventually passed through a military checkpoint and into a tribal zone still uncontrolled by the Pakistani government. We could have increased our firepower in the tribal zone, as we were offered anything from a muzzle-loader to a machine gun for a minimal price. Charlie was at home here, but our liaison officer refused to get off the bus. When darkness fell, Charlie stopped for mealtime where men were gathered in a cave by the road cooking flatbread on stones over a fire. We gathered around, thinking it was unwise for our health to eat there. One man would tear off a chunk of the large round of bread, then pass it to the next, who tore off a chunk, passed it two more times, and the last chunk, well handled, was passed to me. They were a hard-looking bunch, with big mustaches and ten-inch knives glittering in the firelight. It suddenly seemed unwise for our health to not eat there, so I took the bread, ate it, and thanked them kindly.

I did not think we could sleep through that harrowing night back on the road, but we finally realized that if we were going to die, we were going to die. There was nothing we could do about it. So we crawled on top of our piles of baggage and went to sleep. The next morning we began to get an idea of the astonishing scale of these mountains as we passed Nanga Parbat, the largest escarpment on earth, with a fall line of eighteen thousand feet. We craned our necks to see three and a half vertical miles to the summit. Nearing Skardu, the center of what was once the ancient kingdom of Baltistan, even the sand dunes were fifteen hundred feet high.

When we finally reached Skardu, shaken but still alive, we found a bustling trade center, its dusty streets lined with poplars and skirted with bazaars. Our most pressing task was to hire native Balti porters to help us move our tons of gear to the base of the mountain. Two hundred had lined up in the street, all shouting for a job. To keep the loads at sixty pounds or less, we needed eighty men, but I could not guess if those who shouted loudest could carry the most, or if the quiet ones on the fringes would do the best job. In truth, none of them looked equal to the task—they were small, just over five feet tall, and thin, and ragged. I finally gave up and turned the task over to an experienced sirdar—a native foreman whose job was to make the choice and marshal the porters through the three-day trek. He picked all eighty by name in a minute and a half, and the crowd dispersed.

We stayed the night in Skardu, and the next morning we piled into three topless Land Cruisers with trailers to make the forty-five-mile trip to Askole, the last village at the end of the road. The road, which was more of a trail, was interrupted by frequent landslides, and one slide took over two hours to dig a way through. When one side of the gorge got too steep, we crossed the river on rickety cable suspension bridges floored with old planks, which sagged and swayed as we drove over them. The bridges were considered "strategic military installations," and we were not allowed to photograph them.

We reached Askole in late afternoon to find that the porters we hired in Skardu had amazingly walked through the night and day to meet us here. The village at the edge of the Braldu River was terraced with stacked cobble dwellings dug into the hillside above, and skirted by small fields of buckwheat and apricot groves below. Under the scrutiny of the villagers, we sorted our mountain of baggage into eighty fairly equal piles, and the next morning was a mad scramble among the porters to secure the best loads. It was only then I realized with alarm that the sirdar had included very young and very old porters, neither of which I thought had any business being on our payroll. Among the group was a sixteen-year-old boy, and an eighty-year-old man.

This was the first time we'd had to give up control of the expedition completely. If the porters couldn't get our equipment to the mountain, we could never climb it. How could an eighty-year-old man carry sixty pounds over twenty-five miles of treacherous terrain? I was already angry at the sirdar when one of the porters asked if he could carry a double load for double pay—the load would weigh more than the porter! Before I could say no, the sirdar said yes, and when all the loads were slung and the porters filed up the trail beside the Braldu River, I stepped in behind the one with the double load to make certain he would keep up. I was carrying ten pounds—a jacket, water, and lunch. After two hours I could barely see him far ahead; by lunchtime I couldn't see him at all, and when the old men breezed by me on the trail, they were singing.

Our "elite" team of American climbers was here the weakest link, I realized. I had made the mistake of judging these porters based on what I believed they could do. According to my experience, they did not appear equal to the task. But the Balti people, Tibetan by ancestry, are a product of the Karakoram Himalayas, and nobody could be more equal. The occasional blue-eyed porters were reminders of old collisions with other peoples, like

Alexander the Great, who was stopped in his tracks by the fierceness of their attacks followed by sudden retreats into the inaccessible heights. Lines were never drawn through their country, only around it.

I was further educated when I later spoke to the eighty-year-old Hussein. He told me he had been a porter for the first successful expedition to K2 in 1954, that he had a sixty-year-old son who was also a porter, and a second son who was a porter and forty-eight, and a third son who was eight years old! When we eventually reached the glacier, old Hussein took off his shoes to walk barefoot, and when I asked him why, he said, "Because glaciers are very hard on shoes."

As we walked up the Braldu River gorge, we passed beneath jagged mountains that shot up eight thousand feet above the river, terrain that would have dwarfed the Alps. When I asked the porters what were the names of these mountains, they shrugged. They had no names; these were only the foothills. At the end of the second day we reached Paiju Camp, the last vegetation before the world turned glacial. Here were both trekkers and climbers going up the Baltoro to K2, and we spent a sociable evening sharing stories by the campfires. When we said good-bye and good luck the next morning, it would be the last time we would see them.

Our porters picked up their loads, and we left the hectic bustle of Paiju Camp, moving ahead toward the mighty bulk of the Baltoro Glacier. The ice stretched a mile across the valley, captured between walls of polished granite that rose precipitously, two miles and more above the turbulent glacier. The beginning of the Braldu River crashes out of an ice cavern in the glacier's face, milky with sediment and born fully grown. The trail picked a way up the carved face of ice to the glacier's surface, which was strewn with a chaos of rock and debris from the mountains above. It looked, as Galen Rowell once described it, "as if God's own construction company had run out of funds and left the scene incomplete."

In places the rubble gave solid footing, and the trail, which changed by year and season with the glacier's movement, followed the surest path. But we had to leave the path after only a mile, because our destination was crosswise from the trend, turning up the Trango Glacier. There would be no more footsteps to follow, and our sirdar scouted a route for the porters, weaving across the waves of ice with their rocky crests and canyon crevasses. Despite the sirdar's care, the porters slipped frequently down into the icy troughs, and I no longer wondered why they stopped to say prayers before they set foot on the malevolent river of ice.

We arrived at last at the confluence of the Trango Glacier, where its meeting with the dominant Baltoro was argued in groans and deep sighing moans as ice ground against ice. The turbulence of that right-angled collision slowed our progress even further. It felt to me like we had been crawling all day, but I was secretly glad we could not move any faster. I had woken up that morning with the realization that time no longer insulated us—by the end of the day we would meet our mountain. As we picked our way between ice and rock, I could almost hear the drumbeats. My teammates were silent. There had been no joking this morning, and little lightheartedness.

As we climbed up to the surface of the Trango Glacier, we were feeling the first real strains of altitude. We had begun the day at eleven thousand feet and were now approaching fifteen thousand. We had to cross the half-mile breadth of Trango Glacier, down and up the parallel cracks cut like gullies in the ice. We reached the far side and clung to the edge of Great Trango, the blocky member of the Trango group, sidling along its giant bulk to avoid the ice. The massive buttress blocked any view of our mountain, but in the precipitously vertical nature of this world, Great Trango ended suddenly.

We turned a corner and there it was. The buttress dropped away, and Trango Tower rose stunningly before us. "Tower," "monument," even "skyscraper" were insignificant words to describe the monolithic size of this granite block honed vertical by glacial ice. A moment before we had known the mountain only as a picture—palm-sized, two-dimensional, a mere postcard of a dream. The reality hit us like a shock wave. We stopped dead in the middle of the track, and the porters had to step around us.

Each patted us on the back in passing, for no amount of bluff or bravado could hide the fact that we were absolutely horrified.

We stood and stared, speechless, and finally stumbled after the porters, who had arrived at a small lake at the bottom of the mountain's slope where they were dropping their loads at what would become our Base Camp. We paid the porters, giving each an extra day's wage because they had given us a native way to think about the Himalayas. We kept two porters to help shuttle loads, and a cook for Base Camp, and the rest filed happily away back down the glacier.

We sorted through the packs that evening and set our tents up mutely. The small lake surrounded by rising rock made a reflecting pool to look into as the Himalayan light faded pink, then blue-black. I went to bed that night, but I could not sleep. How were we *ever* going to climb this mountain? We had prepared ourselves to come here, but we were not prepared for what we found. The mountain was too high, too vertical, just too damned much. We might be some of the best wall climbers in the world, but that didn't mean we were good enough.

That first stunning view of Trango Tower was burned on my mind as I rolled back and forth in my sleeping bag. It was almost with relief that I heard Jeff in the darkness, tapping on the thin nylon of the tent. "Todd, are you awake?" But then he followed with, "Steve's not feeling good." My stomach sank another notch.

"What's wrong?"

"He's got a splitting headache. It's so bad now we've got to do something."

I got up immediately. Headaches are common at high altitude, but they usually go away. Steve's had been getting worse for three days, and he was losing his balance and vision. The best cure for altitude sickness is a rapid descent, and we had brought along a hyperbaric bag, which inflates around a person to simulate the increased pressure of a lower altitude, a lifesaving device for Himalayan climbers. Under the light of our headlamps, we dug the bag out of our pile of gear, helped Steve into it, and began pumping.

We effectively lowered Steve's altitude by seven thousand feet, but by morning he still wasn't feeling better. We had to conclude that altitude was not the problem, which meant we still didn't know what was. If you can't diagnose an illness, you can't treat it. If you don't treat an illness here, the consequences can be deadly.

We all gathered in council and glumly agreed that Steve had to get out, and fast. He couldn't go alone, so Jeff would go with him, back to Askole, back to Skardu, back to Islamabad, and we presumed back to the States. It turned out that Steve had a sinus infection, and the doctors said if he hadn't come out for treatment he could have died. It was the correct decision, but it wasn't an easy one.

We watched them walk away, the three of us who were left. And while our mountain hadn't gotten any bigger, we felt infinitely smaller standing under it. If it weren't for Steve, I would not have found a team to come here. Steve believed strongly in the dream, shoring up my own doubts, and Mike and Bobby believed in part because Steve did. He had brought the wonderful impetus of youth, with its reckless impatience that says let's go now and seize the moment. He was the known element on my team, a steadfast and tenacious partner. With that leg kicked out, we wobbled now precariously.

We were facing at this point the critical transition from preparation to action, from the horizontal to the vertical. Years of dreaming, planning, and training had brought us to this point, but we did not know how we could take the next step. Two out of five team members were gone, as well as the porters, leaving four thousand pounds of gear behind that could not easily be moved back out. Our mountain loomed overwhelmingly above us, and the odds of our success sank beneath it.

We were apprehensive because there was so much we didn't know, and hesitant about taking the first step on the climb. Why begin when we had so little hope of achieving our end? We had a good excuse to leave now, before we tried and failed. So many unexpected things had worked against us, some of it just plain bad luck, and no one would blame us if we turned around now. The shock of our first view had not lessened overnight, and, in truth, more than apprehensive, more than uncertain, we were afraid.

17. If you are not afraid, you have probably chosen too easy a mountain.

To be worth the expedition, to field a team to climb this mountain, it had better be intimidating. If you don't stand at the base uncertain how to reach the summit, then you have wasted the effort to get there. A mountain well within your ability is not only a misspending of resources, it is a loss of opportunity across a lifetime of potential achievement.

On an expedition into the unknown, there is always a difference between what you have prepared for and what you find, and the magnitude of that difference is often unnerving. When your mountain is suddenly in front of you, larger and more impossible than you had imagined, it is a shock that makes you reel. That shock for us had been amplified by our sudden and proximate view. If we had been able to see our mountain for fifty miles, growing gradually larger in front of us, we would have had time to prepare more, to slowly accept the size of our challenge. As it was, we could not take our eyes off the mountain that first day.

But there is a validation that comes with sheer terror, because you know then that you are playing in an ultimate arena. Fear, uncertainty, doubt, and dismay are all signal markers of a Himalayan-sized mountain, of a goal, worthy of your desire to climb. If you have stood below high mountains in the past, you recognize this fear as an old friend. It's like the samurai who runs to hug the opponent he is about to fight, because without a great challenger, he would not have approached the perfection of his skills.

Being afraid shows that you are crossing the frontier edge of your comfort zone, and right where it starts to get uncomfortable is where you begin to grow. The discomfort of fear is normal when you are facing an ultimate mountain, and when you recognize that, you can adapt more quickly. Fear can be energizing and doesn't have to be a negative emotion if you understand that it is a natural response to challenges—the greater the fear, the greater the challenge. Employ that energy toward achieving the goal instead of using it as an excuse to turn away.

A large part of the fear we felt was caused by uncertainty. When you stand at the base of a mountain like Trango Tower, you only know one thing: that you don't know all the answers. But remember you are there to learn the answers. If you knew everything you were taught in college before you ever went, there would be no reason to seek knowledge there. If you already knew how to climb this mountain, you could gain nothing from the ascent and would, in fact, lose the opportunity of learning something on a harder mountain. That willingness to learn allows a large leap forward when you are stepping into the unknown.

While fear and uncertainty were our first responses to the mountain looming above us, that was followed almost immediately by doubt. It was painfully obvious that we were not good enough to climb it. We might have made a reconnaissance trip the year before to see what we were getting into, to be better prepared, to answer some of the questions. But if any of us had actually laid eyes on the mountain before, we wouldn't have come back to climb it. Not this year, and maybe never. We would not have believed we could ever become good enough.

And while we knew that altitude would make the climb more difficult, we weren't prepared for how hard it was just to breathe at fifteen thousand feet in Base Camp doing nothing. What would it be like at twenty thousand feet trying to hang on to an edge with feet dangling? And we discovered to our dismay that the headwall at the top of the tower was overhanging, and the last rope lengths of the climb would be the hardest. No one had told us that, which made me angry until I realized the experts gave us a dozen reasons not to come here and had dozens more if I had asked for them.

I understand now that instead of viewing fear and doubt as

signs that you shouldn't have come, you should see them as green lights to greater achievement. Complacency and business-as-usual routine are the real red lights to progress. Opportunity always arrives with uncertainty, and uncertainty marks the first step on the path to reward.

But that first full day in Base Camp I kept looking up at the overhanging headwall, then down in dismay. And every time I gasped for breath I thought, *The higher we go, the worse it's going to get*. We had come as prepared as we were going to be, but the mountain was beyond us. How could we ever begin to become equal to it? Fear and doubt are often followed by the desire to turn back, or the propensity to lower your objective in order to raise your odds of success, and these are more dangerous crevasses than the real ones that block your passage.

The transition between preparation and action, from horizontal to vertical, is always difficult, because you are poised but not yet propelled. If you don't make that transition with the right mindset, the expedition will be over before the climb has begun. Your attitude at the point you start to climb sets the tone for the entire ascent. It is much easier to begin with the right attitude than to correct your attitude once you have begun. You want to leave the ground with as little unnecessary weight as possible, and to do that you must look into your backpack to see what burdens are lurking there.

18. The specter of the mountain can loom larger than the mountain itself.

In your first view of new terrain, even the foothills look higher than any mountains you have seen. The overwhelming challenge, unexamined, can exceed your belief that you can rise to meet it. Under the shadow of the mountain, you must overcome your paralysis with analysis to understand your apprehen-

sions. The weight of the specter can be left behind, but only if you consciously leave it there.

Your first view of the mountain may give you pause, but if you pause too long, inertia will undermine your momentum. There is often a kind of prebattle paralysis at the base of a mountain, like stage fright before the curtain lifts, when the imagination is overwhelmed by everything that could go wrong. If you were only there to view the mountain, like an audience at the play, you would not feel apprehension and doubt. But you are there to climb the mountain, and the unpredictability of that future action forms a specter that looms larger than the mountain itself.

The specter of the mountain casts a heavy shadow made up of uncertainty, the weight of unanswered questions, and the overwhelming nature of the challenge before you. The goal appears unachievable, and unchallenged assumptions can become perceived as truths. The weight of the specter unchallenged will affect your performance and can be dangerous because it fuels the urge to turn back.

When you see the whole of the mountain before you—the avalanche-swept approach, the icy, twisted base, the overhanging headwall, and the razor summit a mile above—you cannot imagine how to climb it all, and what might happen on the way. If you start up with the weight of the specter in your backpack, you will stagger under the load. You must empty your pack and sort out what is real from what is magnified. Reasoned analysis can reduce the specter of the mountain by isolating each element and considering them in turn.

On any expedition, the unknowns can potentially stop you, and in climbing, they can also kill you. You can't ignore any of them. But you can sort them by priority and probability. If I am afraid of the overhanging headwall, analysis will tell me that I can't yet climb a stretch of rock thousands of feet above me, just as I cannot stand on a ledge two years in the past. A mountain can only be climbed a rope length at a time, and understanding that allows you to reduce the complexity and magnitude of the larger formula.

If I am afraid of falling rocks, analysis will point out that rocks fall more during certain times of the day, and I can lessen my risk by adjusting my schedule. Once isolated, the issues that need immediate attention should get immediate attention, and what may be a problem in the future must be dealt with in its turn. Real resources must be allocated only to real problems.

The desire to retreat is a common response to an overwhelming challenge. But if you do not counteract this urge, even if you start upward, you will soon come down because where the mind goes the body will follow. I can name countless expeditions that failed for this reason, expeditions that had adequate or even surplus supplies, climbing skill, time, and good weather. Many of the real difficulties had already been overcome, and the rest were overcomable. But the team started up with such trepidation that their progress was merely an interruption of their retreat.

We would have been supported for a decision to leave Trango Tower before we even started, given the disadvantages we faced. No one is ever criticized for leaving a Himalayan mountain while they are still alive. To view the beast, then go home to sharpen our swords, would have been a prudent course of action, everyone would agree. The Himalayas give you countless real reasons to leave on any given day, and you can invent countless more.

We tried instead to define our fears and analyze their probability, so we could carry in our backpacks only what we needed. And the longer we stayed in unfamiliar terrain, the lighter our packs became, because part of the weight of the specter is its newness. The mind responds only to a certain amount of stimulus, even if it's horror, before it recalibrates itself to horror as the norm. By the second day, we found ourselves looking up less often as we sorted our piles of gear in anticipation of beginning the climb.

But the specter of the mountain is not the only excess weight in your backpack. You also carry doubt in your ability to become equal to the mountain. It may be beyond you, but if you don't believe that you can grow to meet the challenge, you cannot begin to leave the ground.

19. What you do not know, the mountain will teach you.

> Your first reaction to an ultimate mountain is that you are not equal to the challenge, so you might as well go home. You could then train harder, prepare more, and come back another year. But the truth is that there is nowhere else to train but on this mountain. By definition, you are not good enough, because the challenge is something harder than you've ever done, but that doesn't mean you can't become good enough. The improvement you need to reach the summit can only be gained on your way to the summit.

When you set out to climb a mountain that has never been climbed, a mountain that embodies a new level of achievement, you will realize at the base that you don't know how to get to the summit. But no amount of preparation before you arrive will give you all the answers. Each new mountain is like higher education: the classroom moves upward with every lesson you learn, and the teacher revealing if your answers are right or wrong is the mountain itself.

The attempt of something improbable is often the richest learning environment, and the most accelerated way to improve. A major-league baseball player won't gain much by practicing with the Little League, but think how much a Little League player would improve in the opposite situation. An elevated playing field brings elevated results.

Intrepidness—a willingness to go wherever the answers can be found—is another of the essentials to carry in your Personal Backpack. It includes both the belief that you have something valuable to learn, and the action of seeking answers wherever they might be. When you know all the answers, your world is a very comfortable place. Old dogs can learn new tricks, they just don't like to because it means their world has suddenly become less comfortable. Here is a question they don't know the answer to.

The discomfort of not knowing all the answers often keeps people away from new terrain, which in turn reinforces the belief that they already know everything they need to know. A willingness to continue learning expands your field of opportunity and increases the breadth and depth of questions that can be asked. Instead of being comfortable by having all the answers, take comfort in the search for answers.

To actively seek answers, you must go to where the answers can be found, not wait and wonder what the answers might be, not hope they will be handed to you. The door is open, but you must cross the threshold to find out what is on the other side. Each answer is another step up the mountain, which allows you to ask the next question. The most successful climbers don't have more answers to begin with, but are simply more willing to look for the answers, and, more important, to keep asking the questions.

The unknown is like a magnet that both attracts and repels. Fear and discomfort turn us back because we don't see a beaten path to lead us to our destination. An anticipation of reward pulls us forward toward the clues that one by one unveil the solution. When you set out with the belief that the answers are out there, and all you need to do is go to look for them, it is easier to begin to make a path where no footprints show the way. If you have chosen the right mountain, you will know at the base that you are not a good-enough climber to get to the top. You climb the mountain to become good enough.

On an ultimate mountain, there is never a guarantee of success. One section of blank rock, one answer that cannot be found, might end the ascent before you reach the summit. It is always a gamble—one in which you try every conceivable way to stack the odds in your favor, but still a gamble. It is often that lack of a guarantee that you will reach the summit that keeps you from starting with the commitment that will allow you to reach the summit.

20. To succeed you have to be willing to risk failure.

It is often difficult to start climbing a mountain once you are at the base because of the very vivid visualization of what will happen if you don't succeed. If you never start, then that is your excuse. You did not fail because you did not begin. You don't have to be willing to fail, but to achieve the gain that comes with leaving the ground, you must be willing to risk failing.

Standing at the base of Trango Tower, I wanted to turn back, because I knew we were not good enough. Only in retrospect did I realize that there was no place we could have trained, no other challenge that would approximate the one before us. The other mountains we had climbed only tricked us into coming here. They did not prepare us to climb this mountain, they only prepared us to make the decision to climb it. But I knew instinctively that even if we had every reason in the world to leave, we had to stay. If you do not stay, you cannot begin the process of succeeding.

Fear of failure is in some ways more daunting than fear of the unknown. You are seldom criticized for retreating from the unknown—who knows what dangers might have lurked there? But to begin a mountain and then not reach the summit is by external definition a failed expedition. The only way to avoid the risk of failure is to climb mountains well within your ability, or never leave the ground at all.

The alternative is to manage both the risk and your fear. You can manage risk by applying strategies to enhance your success at each stage of the expedition. To manage your fear you must put that fear in perspective. Every step up the mountain is a success to be celebrated. You might argue that if we stayed but failed to reach the summit, we did not ultimately succeed. But remember that success is gained incrementally with each small gain toward the summit.

The summit defines the end of the immediate goal, but the goal of your Lifelong Ascent is to become a more capable climber, and that is achieved by the process of climbing itself. On an ultimate mountain, there is no failure unless you turn away from the challenge when you can still continue climbing. You have chosen the mountain for maximum gain, and even if you fail to reach the summit, you achieve significantly more than you would by reaching the summit of a moderate mountain, and infinitely more than if you never left the ground.

The definition of failure is often assigned by external sources according to their expectations. How many times have we seen an Olympic athlete who wins silver declared a failure because they did not win the expected gold, or another wildly celebrated for a bronze because no one thought they could perform so well? The capricious nature of other people's expectations reinforces the need to develop and hold to your own values. When you define for yourself what success is, much of the fear of failure evaporates because you are in control of the ultimate perception of gain.

This brings to mind a software company I spoke to over the course of three years. At its start-up, the owner was blazing with ideas and enthusiasm over the potential of his product. The next year his company was wildly successful, and he was a multimillionaire, but when I saw him at the peak of what others would call success, he seemed bored, listless, and unhappy. The third year, he had sold his company and started a new one, and he was again on fire with enthusiasm. He didn't need to keep working, because he had more money than he could spend. What motivated him was not the summit, but the challenge to reach the summit. To seek the challenge and pursue gain on the way to the summit will always repay the investment. As Saint Gregory said, "The one who would make the true ascent must ascend forever."

At the base of Trango Tower, Bobby, Mike, and I were afraid to begin because we believed there was a good chance we would fail.

Exactly because we were afraid to begin, we began too soon, setting forth to see the elephant. Our third day at Base Camp we started up the mountain to haul a load of supplies to where we would set our next interim camp in the notch below the blocky base of the tower. We wanted to find out what climbing at altitude would be like, and we found out it was hell.

It was only a mile and a half in distance up the gully, but it gained twenty-five hundred feet in elevation. It was a dangerous as well as an exhausting journey that had to be made, up and back, in the four dark hours before daybreak. The first warmth of sunlight would loosen blocks of ice and chunks of rock from all the surrounding walls, which came crashing down in a ricochet from one side of the gully to the other. In daylight we were like ducks in a shooting gallery with all of the mountain gods armed and firing at will.

We were only carrying forty pounds, a moderate weight under normal circumstances, but nothing here was normal. We had been sleeping badly, a hallmark of high altitude because breathing slows during sleep, and oxygen starvation wakes you regularly with violent gasps. What we forced ourselves to eat for breakfast came back up almost immediately. Our muscles would seize up with cramps, like a sprinter who has run one step too far. We nearly had to crawl the last quarter mile to where we emptied our packs, and sat and brooded under the black and overwhelming shadow of the mountain above us.

After fear, doubt, and the desire to retreat, the next dangerous response when facing the wall on an expedition is an inclination to lower your objective. It can manifest itself immediately, or it can overtake you partway up. We could, for example, have decided to climb an easier route, one that had been done before and we knew we could repeat. Or we could have climbed halfway up the mountain and decided at some arbitrary point that, given the difficulty, we had done enough.

But we had chosen our mountain to increase the gradient of our Lifelong Ascent, and we had picked a route that wasn't the easiest way to summit, but was where we would gain the most as climbers. It is true that our mountain was unexpectedly higher than we had imagined, the climbing more difficult, the departure of two-fifths of our team dismaying, and the objective hazards of rock and ice fall daunting. And because of the perceived increase in difficulty, we could in all logic have lowered our objective. But what would we have lost in doing so?

21. You cannot lower the mountain, so you must raise yourself.

If you could cut the mountain in half, you would become half the climber. The mountain remains unalterable. You cannot decrease its size or adjust its geology. You can't turn back the storms or add substance to thin air. The only thing malleable in this equation is your resolve. Your perception of the challenge can be shifted incrementally from uncertainty to resolution, and from apprehension to action. Always adjust the mind to what is possible, do not adjust what is possible to the mind.

You arrive at the mountain uncertain how difficult the climbing will be, and unforeseen setbacks and obstacles beyond your control will only make it harder. Even though you may want to, you cannot say, "I will only climb half the mountain since it is twice as hard as I expected." Because the mountain defines who you can become, lowering the summit will diminish that sum.

At the base of the mountain, you must understand that while the external factors of your challenge can't be changed, the way you perceive the challenge can. You have arrived with time, resources, and manpower—everything is committed here except your most critical asset, which is your mind. Before you take your first step upward, the attitude with which that step is taken has to be examined and solidified. You must believe that the first step will be followed by a second step, and a third, and a three millionth until you reach the top. Every member of your team must carry the same belief. If you do not make this commitment to the summit, even if you move upward, you will eventually turn back.

To raise yourself to the challenge, you should first acknowledge the value in doing so. Why leave the ground at all? Knowing why you are there validates the effort you are about to make and illuminates the path ahead. Second, you should empty everything out of your backpack you don't need, including the specter of the mountain, resistance to learning in a new environment, and your fear of failure. Third, make sure the things you originally brought are still in your backpack—your compass, the habit of ascent, a frontier mentality, your unified sense of mission, intrepidness, and another asset you may not realize you still have—the momentum you packed at the beginning when you made the decision to climb this mountain, which grew with the assembled team and has carried you this far. This may be the first step on the climb, but on the expedition it is simply the next step, and knowing that makes the step easier to take.

To be able to take the next step, you must divide the mountain into manageable parts. Climbing is a process, both in its physical movement of one hand and foot above the other, and in its mental calculation of applying the right resources at the right time. It is problem solving at its purest because every movement asks a new question, and the answer is either right, and you move upward, or it is wrong and you come back down. The larger expedition to climb the mountain, from the dream to the choice of team, from the preparation to the approach, from the first step to the last, is also a process. You cannot climb the mountain all at once, and you must break it into steps or you cannot begin.

It isn't always the difficulty of the climbing that makes you wish you could lower your objective. Conditions can become worse, setbacks might slow your ascent, hazards can appear suddenly, and the climb becomes proportionately more uncertain of outcome. But an increase in adversity should not automatically trigger a decrease in aspiration. Adversity should be treated like an adversary that calls upon you to rise, not as a reason to quit climbing.

"Adversity" and "adversary" come from the same root word, and though we often perceive them differently, they are part of the same package. Playing football against your archrival is a contest with an adversary. Playing that same game in a raging blizzard is adversity. But you cannot separate the snow from the game—it is one more element that makes your goal harder to reach, but the game goes on whether (and weather) you like it or not. Whichever competitor reacts most positively to this adversity increases their odds of winning the game.

Our adversaries help to define us, both in the amount of energy we invest, and the skills we attain to triumph in the contest they provide. What would a superhero be without his arch nemesis? Every sports team has one rival they want to beat more than the others, and they try harder to do it. A runner might do battle with a ticking clock; a salesman stands up against an impossible number. An adversary doesn't have to be a person or an opponent, it is simply a declared challenge that asks for your best in response.

If you do not have an adversary, you should create one. Name your summit, and like a mountain of granite, the solidity of that summit can motivate you like nothing else, because it pulls you upward in answer to the challenge. Whenever you feel that you would like to make your adversary half of who or what they are, you have forgotten how they define you. Half the mountain makes you only half the climber.

Because we don't plan for it, adversity, the cousin of our friend adversary, often appears like a handicap, an unfair burden that decreases our odds of success. We curse the blizzard, the downturn in the market, how the hardest climbing is near the top of the mountain where we are weariest. While adversity, like your adversary, increases the level of your challenge, it also increases your capacity to succeed in the future. To treat adversity as something separate and outside of the contest is to look for an excuse to call off the game. Use adversity as a trigger to increase your resolve. Play anyway. Laugh in the face of the storm. There is glory in the difficulty, and courage in the quest.

When you are facing the wall, everything will conspire to stop you. Immobility is easy. Rising above that immobility is hard. But your backpack has been emptied of all unnecessary weight, and filled with the tools of a frontier ascent. You have come to this mountain to climb it, and that act is momentum itself. A sage friend once distilled the spirit of ascent. "I have striven for the icy summits all of my life. I have not failed because I have not ceased."

5. CROSSING DIFFICULT TERRAIN

How to Fall Toward the Summit

We rested a day after our first haul up the gully, then carried a second load. With little photographing to do at that point, Bill Hatcher helped us set our next interim camp at 17,500 feet. We pinned one small, two-man mountain tent tightly behind a large boulder near the crowning notch of the gully leading up to the base of Trango Tower, and another tent was perched inconveniently on a sloping ledge 150 feet to the side. The boulder provided our only shelter from rock and ice chunks careening down the gully, and standing to the side of the boulder's perpetual shadow was a dangerous proposition. The walls rose up so precipitously on either side of the canyon that sunlight warmed the camp for a single hour in the late afternoon. For the rest of the day, it was uncomfortably cold with a narrow, claustrophobic view.

We spent the next night at that Notch Camp and decided it was not a pleasant place to live. Crouching behind the boulder on shifting talus to melt dirty snow for water, we were exhausted after a day climbing the thousand-foot blocky base of Trango to fix ropes for a regular commute. From then on, we would use ascenders to jumar up the fixed ropes and speed our passage, but speed was a relative term because it took hours of slow, labored movement to gain that thousand feet.

It was a devious route, twisting back and forth across the staircase of rock, which meant we could not haul freight in one vertical line using our body weight to bring the bags up on pulleys. Instead we would have to pack supplies on our backs and climb with the extra weight, an exhausting prospect at this altitude. The next day we made that haul up the fixed ropes, and it was one of the most miserable experiences we had ever faced. We were going too high too fast, but the same reaction to the fear of beginning that had propelled us to Notch Camp was pushing us higher still. We took cold comfort in the fact that this would be the easiest climbing on the mountain.

At the top of the blocky base of Trango, at 18,500 feet, we found a narrow ledge at the edge of a steeply sloping snow field on the shoulder leading to the main wall. The ledge was seven feet wide by twenty-five long, defined abruptly on one side by a thousand-foot drop, and sheltered on the other side by overhanging rock. It seemed a tentative perch, exposed and confining at the same time, but there was no other even remotely safe place to put our next camp. Above us loomed the two-thousand-foot main wall of Trango Tower, below us a staggering free fall to the glacier, and to every side mountains among the highest in the world, carved into pinnacles and broken with ridges, highlighted by fields of snow and underlined with snaking glaciers.

We set up two small tents on our thinly defined ledge, each so close to the edge that you could not walk to the outside of it without stepping off into space, which left barely a path to walk to the inside, with a mere five steps between tents. This eagle's perch was not meant for the wingless, but we had to light somewhere. Uneasy with the thought of spending much time here, it was with relief that we started back down to Notch Camp, joking about how nobody better start sleepwalking at that Shoulder Camp. When we finally arrived back at Base Camp after three days of getting the interim camps set, it felt like a four-star hotel in comparison.

We continued to shuttle loads from Base Camp to Notch Camp, and from Notch Camp to Shoulder Camp, always returning to Base Camp at night because Himalayan wisdom dictated "Carry high, sleep low." That was the one rule we had come with, a tool in our backpack we had been handed and didn't dare not carry with us. Lowering your elevation helps you to recover from the effects of altitude, as well as increases your margin of safety, but it was a full day's commute to get from Base Camp to Shoulder Camp, where the harder climbing began, and the trip was exhausting. How could we make that thirty-five-hundred-vertical-foot approach day after day *and* climb the rest of the mountain?

We had originally planned on rotating teams back to Base Camp, since only one person at a time can actually lead the rope upward while a second belays, leaving the other two free. But now we were a team of three. Because the altitude took so much out of our endurance, we all would probably have to take turns leading the rope higher on any given day. And there was so much work to do besides the climbing—loads of supplies to carry up, and the basic chores of staying alive. How would we decide who would go down to Base Camp, and when, and for how long?

We were discussing this problem at Shoulder Camp, after having hauled up a forty-pound load each, when the only solution became evident, whether we liked it or not. None of us could go back to Base Camp. We would have to get the two remaining porters to haul loads for us to Notch Camp, and every few days one of us could drop down to Notch Camp and bring a load up to Shoulder Camp. But we would not return to Base Camp again until the climb was finished. This thin ledge clinging to the edge of the vertical world, so insubstantial and tenuous, would have to become home from now on.

We thought we had started up the mountain with the bare minimum in our backpacks, but this one tool of Himalayan wisdom we had brought with us, this dictum to return to Base Camp as often as possible, had to be discarded. To climb this mountain, we could not carry the weight of a tool that wouldn't work. We had to eliminate the commute and live with the difficulties. This is where the hard climbing began, and living down in Base Camp isolated us both physically and mentally from the mountain we were going to climb. Not only was the commute too resource-consuming, but every time we arrived back at Shoulder Camp it seemed a foreign and hostile place. The surest way to make it more familiar was to stay.

22. Living with the difficulties makes you at home in the extreme.

As you rise on a mountain, conditions become increasingly hostile and alien. When you arrive at a place so unfamiliar, you feel out of your element. But if you go down again to safety, when you come back the next day you will still feel out of your element. To perform at a high level in a new environment, you must spend the time there to make that environment feel like home.

A hostile environment might be defined as any place you feel uncomfortable, and when you are uncomfortable, you don't perform as well—the more attention you must give to your discomfort, the less you have left to give to everything else. The quicker you can adapt to a hostile environment and the more comfortable you feel there, the better you perform. The "home court advantage" comes largely from the comfort of a familiar environment, and you want to develop that home court advantage wherever you go so you don't continually feel the disorientation and disadvantage of the visiting team.

Discomfort always has a physical expression—we all know what it feels like to be uncomfortable—and sometimes it has a physical cause: we're too cold or too hot, thirsty, hungry, or tired. But often it is an emotional response to the unexpected or unfamiliar: new terrain, a new challenge or new level of the same challenge. The more these separate factors are combined, the more uncomfortable we feel. To be cold, hungry, thirsty, and tired in a completely unfamiliar place, facing an unexpected, new, and extreme challenge is about as uncomfortable as you can get.

Physical discomfort, while not always immediately resolvable, does have an obvious solution: if you are hungry, you feed yourself; if you're cold you increase your clothing or improve your shelter. But emotional discomfort is harder to resolve, and requires less obvious modes of adaptation. We all have a survival instinct to move away from what makes us umcomfortable, but if we seek the rewards of higher ground, it often means we must move into a hostile environment to gain what we seek.

When you are facing a hostile environment, the surest way to gain a sense of comfort is to stay in the place that makes you uncomfortable, to confront your fears, to repeatedly do the thing you don't want to do until you wonder what the big deal was. If we didn't sleep well in a mountain tent on a tiny ledge with a thousand-foot drop, we would never learn to sleep well there by returning to Base Camp every night. To move toward your Ultimate Potential, you have to occupy the unfamiliar. To advance the team, you have to advance the team's home field.

To increase your rate of adaptation, it is helpful to analyze which of the factors is causing your discomfort. Are you uncomfortable because the terrain is new? Because the level of challenge has increased? Because you are cold? What isn't unfamiliar in the environment? When we looked at our situation at Shoulder Camp, we realized there weren't that many things we were unfamiliar with. We were used to sleeping in mountain tents. We were familiar with being a long way off the ground. We had weathered many mountain storms. Yes, this was extreme, we told ourselves, but not that much more extreme.

The most immediate way to gain a sense of comfort is, of course, to carry "home" wherever you go. I've always liked the Thoreau quote: "Rest . . . by many brooks and hearth-sides without misgiving. . . . Rise free from care before the dawn, and seek adventures. Let the noon find thee by other lakes, and night overtake thee everywhere at home. There are no larger fields than these, no worthier games than may here be played." To believe in your ability to adapt to any situation makes that adaptation happen much more quickly.

And remember that discomfort slides on a scale of relativity. I've seen climbers at the base of Half Dome who were miserable because they were a two-hour hike away from a shower and a bed. And I've seen my uncle Courtney spend the night out in a blizzard without batting an eye. How you define discomfort is always relative to your experience with discomfort. The more you endeavor into hostile terrain, the more comfortable you become with the process of adapting, and the more you realize that discomfort is only temporary.

You can extend the boundaries of your own relative scale by continually looking for opportunities to move beyond your comfort zone, by not refusing to go where conditions are different than you are used to. An expanded scale of relative comfort is an asset to carry in your backpack and can be gained not only from your own experience, but from observing people who appear comfortable where you are not. A team can take its cue from the most comfortable member and raise the scale of all to the level of one.

When we made the decision to stay at Shoulder Camp, the implications were frightening because that decision went against everything we had been led to believe was true. We didn't know what strategy *would* work, only what wouldn't work. But we also felt like a huge weight had been lifted off us because we no longer had to think about the lower part of the mountain. We could consolidate the gains we had made, and all our energy now was focused upward. And while the challenge never got any easier—with the mountain less steep or the camp less exposed—each morning we woke up a little less afraid. We were becoming Trango Tower natives, and gaining the advantage of the home team.

The climbing proved surprisingly strenuous, up thin cracks running like lasers for hundreds of feet. A 5.11 at this extreme altitude required much more effort than a 5.12 or even 5.13 at sea level, and the first three pitches—a straight crack leading to a traverse over to a chimney, followed by another series of cracks that ended at two wobbly blocks resembling giant rabbit ears—were all hard 5.11. One of our greatest difficulties was that altitude required us to change our style of climbing. Holding on to the rock with two hands tightens the chest muscles so you cannot breathe deeply, a situation you can quickly recover from at low altitude. But here we had to breathe constantly and deeply just to suck in enough oxygen to keep from passing out, so we could only climb a short distance using both hands, then we had to find a solid hold and swing one arm out to open the chest cavity and catch our breath. It made the climbing both choppy and slow.

After three days of working on the beginning of the route, Mike and Bobby asked how long I thought it would take to finish the climb. They looked to me as the authority on big walls, and I knew they weren't just asking how much patience and tenacity would be required, but how heavily we needed to supply Shoulder Camp. Would it be a sprint or a marathon? Nine days was the longest time any team I heard of had spent living on a Himalayan wall. I looked up, thought about the distance and the logistics of covering that distance, assumed that the climbing wouldn't be much harder than 5.11, added a few days for bad weather, and said, "Fifteen days."

Fifteen days seemed like forever in this hostile environment, where each day felt like a week, but I believe that bad news early is good news, because it gives you time to accept the facts and move on. Bad news concealed till the last minute creates a crisis that is harder to recover from. I presented the fifteen days as a worst-case scenario, and my teammates swallowed hard, nodded, and began the mental march toward that distant sum.

We were all working extremely well as a team now. Whoever wasn't connected to the rope dropped down to Notch Camp to bring up a load, or melted snow for water, cooked, sorted gear—whatever they saw would advance the effort toward the summit. I attribute the growing success of our teamwork to the fact that the team had been invested in the goal from the beginning—we all had incentive to succeed. But, more important, I had never asserted that I was the leader, that all decisions had to be cleared through me, that I would give assignments detailing what had to be done and who would do it. I knew this couldn't be *my* expedition or we would never reach the top. To succeed at all that needed to be done, to generate the commitment, the initiative, and the heroism required, it had to be *our* expedition.

23. The more unyielding the mountain is, the more flexible the leadership model must become.

To succeed on an ultimate mountain, every team member must contribute their best effort wherever it is needed. A rigid organization of authority and assigned responsibilities can limit contribution. Leadership and responsibility should be shared, allowing whoever is in the best position to advance the team toward the summit to take the lead on a moving front.

Because you are crossing unknown terrain, answers will not be given to you, but must be sought, and sought by everyone on the team. To successfully find the answers as quickly as possible, the team cannot be constrained by either rank or job description, but must be allowed to move both vertically and laterally in the search. The strict military model of leadership, with its pyramid of stratified rank and compartmentalized jobs, does not work effectively in this environment exactly because it lacks the malleability to adapt instantly to changing conditions, and it doesn't encourage all members to rise to match the mountain.

The military model of leadership obviously has its advantages. It is easy to organize, there is always someone who can be held accountable, it is orderly and disciplined, members can get promoted through the ranks to gain traditional currency, and it is perfectly adequate for repeatedly climbing moderate mountains. But an ultimate mountain requires more flexibility, and the best way to gain that flexibility is to share leadership among the team.

A leader is anyone who makes a decision that affects the outcome of the expedition, and when everyone takes a leadership role, they all have more invested in the mission and are more likely to succeed. I believe that Shared Leadership is so critical to success on an ultimate mountain that I include it as an essential to carry in the Expedition Backpack. If there is one leader, then everyone else is a follower, and followers do not employ the quality and magnitude of initiative needed here.

Leadership should be flexible because you want the person who is in the best position—through expertise, ability, or opportunity—to take the lead whenever they can move the team toward the summit. Because the expedition is moving on many fronts at once, there are multiple opportunities for leadership, and anyone and everyone should be able to fill those openings. A hierarchy of command in that situation is slow, because information has to be passed up and back down (and may no longer be current after it makes that trip), and it is inefficient because so many "middle men" are required.

And because the success of a difficult endeavor requires two parts heart to one part mind, every team member needs a strong degree of ownership and a powerful sense of unified mission, both of which can be subdued by the vertical hierarchy of rank. The military has proven that a person can be ordered to give their life, but they can't be ordered to transcend their life, and transcendence is what you need on an ultimate mountain.

The ability to move laterally is also important, which is why I avoid labeling team members with a job title. Each member of the team has something unique to contribute, and those specialties should be utilized wherever possible. But the team should not be segmented by rigid job descriptions that both excuse members from full participation ("That's not my job!") and exclude them from contribution ("I'd suggest a solution, but I don't want to step on anyone's toes . . ."). A job title is useful because it allows a team member to focus on what they do best, but it can also become a box they can't or won't step out of, even if that step will clearly advance the team.

An added benefit of the shared leadership model is that exceptional performance is reinforced within the team. Equality among the players encourages all to play better, because their teammates are counting on them. When all have an equal stake in the goal, the achievement of one team member doesn't mean the checkmate of another. When one rises, they all rise. This leadership model works best with relatively small teams, and because it works so well within the parameters of a difficult challenge, it is worth dividing a large endeavor into several individual summits that a small team can effectively climb.

The more stratified and segmented an organization is, the less opportunity it has to develop true teamwork, because the structure itself divides people rather than uniting them. An ultimate team moves together toward a defined goal, and everyone on that team has input into the process, an opportunity to affect the outcome, and a reward for making that outcome successful. If you are climbing an ultimate mountain, instead of a job description, agree on a mission description; for a job title, paint EXPEDITION MEMBER on everyone's door.

But if there is no single leader, who makes the decisions, and how are they made? Climbing a mountain is like entering a maze—at every turn you are asked for a decision. The rigid military model of leadership assumes that the person at the top of the pyramid can see into the maze to direct each turn. But in new terrain, the path isn't obvious to anyone. How then is it decided whether to turn left or right?

24. Decisions are made in answer to the mountain.

When you encounter difficult terrain, it becomes very clear that there is no easy path to the summit, but instead a multitude of options each asking for a decision. While the mountain can tell you what remains to be done, it won't reveal the correct answers of how to do it until you test a solution to see if it is right or wrong. To increase your odds of success, options should be discussed by the team, always in reference to reaching the summit. In a shared leadership model, decisions are ultimately made by the person who takes the lead at the time on a particular front, because they have the most real-time data to work from.

A mountain is not as random as a maze, but in some ways the decision-making process is similar—you can't reach the end without making the right choices, and if you make the wrong choice, you have to go back to the exact place you erred to find the correct way. But on a mountain you at least know where the end is. One of the greatest benefits of having defined your summit is that when you reach difficult terrain, the biggest question, "Where are we going?," has already been answered.

The only other question is "How do we get there?" By pre-climbing the terrain in your mind, you can anticipate the twists and turns ahead, and then create an inventory of what stands between you and the summit. That generates a list where you can consistently delete what has been accomplished and reevaluate what remains to be done. If there is uncertainty or dissent among the team over what to do next, the list dictated by the mountain becomes the final authority.

The mountain dictates what needs to be done, but it cannot tell you how to do it prior to the attempted solution. There is no obvious path to the summit, only impressions of possibility. Choose the right one and you move toward the summit; choose the wrong one and you fall back. But the randomness of the choice can be mitigated by the team's collective experience and expertise. We are not rats in a maze—we have foresight, history, and logic in our favor. Facing a difficult decision, a team discussion of which option is most likely to lead to the summit widens the margin for success.

Because you want to move toward the summit, not simply move, decisions must be based not on what you wish were true (or what you feel like you want to do or what would be easiest), but on what will actually advance the team in relation to the summit. As I pointed out earlier, we often make decisions based on the moment, not on the summit. While decisions often have to be made in a moment, they should always be in reference to the goal. The list generated by the mountain can provide a reality check when you make decisions, and the photo of the mountain you have carried with you can improve your perspective when you are standing too close to see the big picture.

Ultimately, decisions of the moment must be made by whoever takes the lead on a moving front. Their information is immediate and constantly changing, their knowledge intimate, and they are in the best position to affect the outcome. If they keep coming down to ask what to do next, they will never get very far up. When everyone is a leader, the team is always advancing, and when the mountain is the final authority, everyone knows where to look for the answers.

Difficult terrain can be daunting to even the best teams, and we were plagued with route-finding problems, false starts, bad weather, and altitude-induced illness. We were paying for our decision to stay at Shoulder Camp with frequent headaches, wobbly stomachs, and a small but daily attrition in strength we were as yet unaware of. But we were being paid back with the focus of thinking only toward the summit, and by a gradual increase in our comfort level and a quicker acclimation to the altitude.

Our climbing days began with the crossing of a 250-yard snow field, forty to one hundred feet wide and sloping steeply to the edge of a thousand-foot drop off the blocky base. Snow was continually sloughing off the edge, and it was a dangerous crossing, because if you slipped, you would not have time to save yourself. We tried roping ourselves together for the crossing, which might have eased our minds but did little for safety, because if one fell he might simply pull the others off with him. We contemplated setting fixed ropes across the snow field, but the safest place to cross provided the least potential for anchors. In the end we simply put on our plastic mountaineering boots and crampons and took one step at a time, alone and carefully. The return crossing was often made after dark when we were tired, which increased the hazard and strain.

When we reached the wall at the base of our route, we took off our boots and socks and put on rock-climbing shoes—sticky rubber-soled slippers we could feel the rock through. Mike and Bobby finally worked out the first 5.11 pitches, and I was trying to find a route higher, but after six long days at Shoulder Camp we had made discouragingly little progress, and the mountain's shadow weighed heavily on our minds. That evening, when we placed our nightly radio call down to Base Camp where our cook, Ali Khan, had taken over management, an unexpected voice came back on the radio. "Jeff? Is that you?" Mike asked. "No, it's John Wayne," he answered flippantly. We thought Jeff was already back in the States with his brother.

And if Jeff was back, that meant Steve was, too. In a split second I was readjusting the formula to include Steve—fresh manpower, more progress, a boost of morale—and suddenly our situation looked infinitely brighter. There was no problem on the mountain that putting Steve back in the mix didn't help with. While my mind was racing, everything else seemed to be happening in slow motion. I reached my hand out for the radio and removed it from the surprised grasp of Mike, brought it slowly toward me, pushed the button in, and said, "Put . . . Steve . . . on!"

"Steve's not here," Jeff answered. "I put him on a plane home." The glittering new light crashed to blackness. It was as if we had been starving on a desert island and a crate landed with FRIED

CHICKEN printed on the side. But when we eagerly broke it open, it was empty. We were suddenly hungrier than if the crate hadn't fallen.

When he signed on to the expedition, Jeff had promised to stick by us to the end of the world, but I thought it was just his bravado talking. We were delighted to have him back, but at the same time we didn't see how he could help us much, and we went to bed thinking gloomy thoughts about our uncertain future. The next morning it began to snow, and continued snowing for three days. "*This* is Himalayan climbing," Mike commented, "or more accurately Himalayan tent sitting."

On the fourth day it cleared enough to shovel three and a half feet of snow off our tiny ledge, but then it snowed again for two more days. Jeff radioed up that an avalanche had wiped out Base Camp. We had set the camp out of the avalanche zone, but did not factor in the massive wind an avalanche generates. Jeff was standing in Base Camp watching this wall of snow tumble down the steep gully, mesmerized by the beauty of the billowing clouds and the rushing, rumbling sound of raw power, when out of the corner of his eye he caught movement. He turned his head and saw the other camp tenders running and then the wall of wind hit him, knocking him flat on his back and covering him with an instant rime of ice crystals.

Some of the tents were flattened, breaking the poles, and others were blown over the ridge or into the small lake where they floated like giant rubber ducks until they were fished out again. It took days for the Base Camp crew to gather and mend and reset the wreckage. It was a potentially serious setback for us, but the way Jeff told the story it was the funniest thing we'd heard in weeks. We needed a little levity at Shoulder Camp, because the climbing wasn't going well. Three pitches up we had to switch cracks, and the traverse between was nearly blank—thin and tenuous, our first 5.13. Between the cold and the altitude, I did not know if it could be done, and I had to focus my attention on rehearsals of that pitch.

We were approaching our fifteen-day "worst case scenario" for completing the climb and were barely a third of the way up the main wall. It was a dark time, full of doubt and frustration. We kept falling at the crux point, right when victory was in sight. And we fell when we least expected it. We fell at the beginning because we were thinking about the end, and we fell half way up. We were finding out what didn't work, and every time we returned to the challenge, we tried to adjust the formula to find out what would work. To cross difficult terrain, you often have to make the wrong choice to discover the right choice. So it isn't the fall that's important, it's what you do after the fall.

25. Falling is not failing.

The most important attitude when leaving the ground in new terrain is to accept that there is a good chance you will fall off. If you don't fall, you might not have gone far enough. Put in place a system of protection to keep your falls from being fatal, and each misstep can accelerate your ascent because you learn more quickly the correct way to climb. If nothing else, falling teaches you in a dramatic way how *not* to climb that particular piece of rock.

When crossing difficult terrain, there is no clear choice of the correct move at the point where you are risking a fall, or you would make it. In a maze you often make a random choice, left or right, and sometimes the correctness of that choice is not evident until many turns later. Climbing a wall, you have a library of movements to draw from, and a contortionist's mastery of body language, so it is an educated guess what the correct answer might be. If you are right you move higher. The wrong answer is dramatically and often instantly pointed out by your rapid descent.

The single hardest decision on a climb is to commit knowing that you may be incorrect, and if you are, you will fall. But you must commit fully because the correct answer applied tentatively could fail, giving you wrong data on the right sequence. Falling is part of the process of learning how to do it right. A guidebook could tell you every correct turn in the maze, but in new terrain you must write your own guidebook, and that endeavor requires you to definitively test answers until you find the one that is right.

We often kick ourselves for being wrong, instead of congratulating ourselves for moving one answer closer to being right. People try to avoid falling for that reason—they equate falling with failing. They don't want to be wrong and are afraid of how others will view their mistakes. But to fear the consequences of a mistake creates a degree of paralysis that could endanger the entire effort. If you are not certain which way to turn, and you can't take the wrong turn to find out, you cannot move from where you are.

That is why it is critical to put in place a system of protection that minimizes or eliminates the negative consequences of a fall. If there is no safety net on a climb, you will never see a bunch of people more afraid of their shadows, and more unwilling to cross the boundary of their abilities. Show me a company culture that punishes any mistake, and I'll show you a company that will go nowhere out in the frontier.

Every time you move into new terrain, you must go as far as you can into the unknown in order to learn what will work, or what might work, or at least to have an indication of what won't work. Being willing to fall on a climb is a tremendous asset, often resulting in getting to the top faster. Falling is not failing because you are not just coming down, you are coming down with valuable information. Even if the attempt is completely wrong, that shows you how not to do it again.

A fall provides you with data from the frontier. It is reconnaissance, and there is no such thing as a failed recon because you always come back with more than you began. Mistakes at the leading edge can be a learning process for the entire team. When you share information gained from the frontier, everyone doesn't have to make the same mistake. The next person into the frontier goes better armed, and in a true team, the setback of one leads to the advancement of all.

When crossing difficult terrain, the goal isn't to not fall, the goal is to find a solution. Falling often brings an acceleration of success, but only if you use what you have learned from one attempt when you make your next attempt.

26. Always fall toward the summit.

When you fall, you have both pushed into the unknown and come back with insight into what lies ahead. But to reach the summit, you must climb beyond the point you fell from. The insight you have gained can be used in a 4A Formula for successfully overcoming obstacles: Attempt a solution to the problem; Analyze what went wrong and right in the attempt; Acquire knowledge and skill from your analysis; and Apply that acquisition to a new attempt.

You are a better climber in the air, while you are falling, than before you fell off, because the fall directs your focus toward improving your performance when you go back up. To gain that improvement, you must analyze precisely what went wrong, make adjustments to the formula, and use the insights you have gained in your next attempt. A 4A Formula for successfully overcoming obstacles can accelerate your progress:

Attempt a solution. Because this is new terrain, nobody knows the answers, so you must make your best guess based on your experience and streaming data. The call to action demands that you try something. The greatest danger on the mountain is to not make a choice, because then you cannot move at all. You also can't wait too long to make the decision, hoping for more information to come to you. Better to risk the fall in pursuit of the answer than to waste time and resources by hesitating too long.

Analyze what went wrong and right. Your analysis at this point has to be very fine. You may have failed in the attempt, but in that failure are the seeds of success. We have a tendency to want to throw the whole machine out when one part is broken. But on the frontier you need to preserve the resources you've got, and that means finding the broken part and fixing what exactly is wrong with the machine. Don't discard what is correct within an incorrect effort. You could be 90 percent right, and without analysis, you might replace that attempt with one that is 90 percent wrong.

The hardest thing to analyze is success. Because it can feel like a gift, we really don't want to look at it too critically. And because it gives us a green light, we often accelerate through the intersection without a second thought. But if we don't analyze success, we haven't learned how to repeat the success. We are trying to take the randomness out of the choice at every turn, so we have more in our backpacks to draw from than simple luck, good or bad.

Acquire knowledge and skill. What you gain from analysis is information and possible solutions to take back up in your next attempt. Without these acquisitions, your ensuing effort will be impeded by the weight of your previous failure. Stung once, you could return in a defensive and tentative manner, and fail from the very fear of failing. To arrive with confidence at the crux point, you must feel like you are better armed, like you are now carrying the key that could unlock the door.

Apply that knowledge to a new attempt. Theories don't climb mountains. These are complex solutions addressed toward the problem of the moment, and you cannot know if your solution is the correct one unless you test it. You are not going home with the information, you are going on. Learn from your mistakes to be able to apply them to the goal. Every time you fall, fall toward the summit.

The 4A Formula is an essential to carry in the Expedition Backpack. It is often a loop instead of a line, regenerated with each unsuccessful attempt until you find the correct sequence. On Trango we applied it repeatedly. We tried placing one hand in the crack and one on a knob to the outside, and when that didn't work, we tried both hands in the crack. We adjusted footholds and changed body positions. We fell off and went back up better armed, and we began to make progress. I decided that if a person gets a medal for anything in this climbing olympics, it ought to be awarded for being willing to fall for the team, not for never falling.

On our fifteenth night at Shoulder Camp, when we had reached our "worst case scenario," Jeff called on the radio and said he was coming up to joins us. "But, Jeff," we called back with concern, "you don't know how to climb the fixed ropes to get here, and this is not the place to learn." We couldn't imagine him even thinking about mastering basic rope work in this environment. According to the Himalayan experts, *we* didn't have enough experience to be up here. What would they say about bringing someone up the wall who had never even tried on a climbing harness?

"I've got all of Steve's gear," he answered, "and if someone doesn't come down and show me how to do it, I'll figure it out for myself."

Despite our reservations, we decided that Mike had better go down the next day and show him how, because we knew that Jeff was a man of his word. Far from intimidated, Jeff was immediately more comfortable on that exposed little ledge than we were. "This is the most laid-back camping trip I've ever been on," he commented. "No hiking, nice camp, great view. You guys have got it pret-ty good." Jeff became Mike's new tentmate and took over the job of hauling loads to supply Shoulder Camp. Sometimes he made two trips a day down to Notch Camp, carrying up fifty pounds a trip in a phenomenal effort. He built stone walls on the outside of the tents and worked daily to make the camp more secure.

And he began to take care of all the housekeeping chores at Shoulder Camp, melting snow, cooking, organizing, which left Bobby, Mike, and me increasingly free to do nothing but climb. Our progress improved significantly, as did our morale. Jeff was always cheerful, pointing out the humorous aspects of our difficulties. And the casual way he dealt with the unfamiliar—whether it was because he had a talent for bringing "home" with him wherever he went, or it wasn't as bad as he expected it to be, or he simply didn't know enough to be afraid—helped extend the scale of our own comfort level.

On the twenty-fifth day, I succeeded on the 5.13 pitch that had haunted us at nineteen thousand feet, and a difficult 5.12 crack that followed. Mike fought his way up an off-width crack the next day, as well as a 5.11 finger crack ending at a big, overhanging block. We were nearing the halfway point on the main wall, and it appeared to us for the first time that barring bad weather, the summit might be attainable.

Not content to be left at camp, Jeff came on up the wall and began belaying us on the higher pitches. Within two weeks of his arrival at Shoulder Camp, the twenty-one-year-old who had never climbed in his life was asking to lead his own pitches. It proved to me that climbing isn't about knowing knots and equipment and technique, it is about the desire to ascend. When Jeff refused to be stopped by what he didn't know, it made the rest of us feel unstoppable.

6. THE STORM

Surviving Serious Adversity

It was the thirtieth day of our stay at Shoulder Camp when Jeff led his first pitch. Before, he had been following ropes that others had led and secured, and it seemed like a bad idea to allow his first attempt to occur at 19,200 feet on the hardest wall in the Himalayas. But Jeff looked at it the way he had looked at everything else—he didn't see a reason why he *couldn't* do it. The pitch was moderate enough that we could have easily climbed it, but Jeff had contributed in every other aspect, and he wanted to contribute in this way as well.

So we gave him a quick lesson in technique and signals, made him practice for half an hour, and when he started up, he immediately forgot everything he had learned. He struggled upward while we anxiously watched, then fell near the top of the pitch, slamming down and swinging on his one correctly placed piece of protection. But on his second try up the pitch he was successful, and we cheered his effort and marveled at his adaptability.

Mike climbed the next pitch to the midpoint of the main wall, marked by pyramid-shaped detached blocks, and it was clear at this juncture that we could no longer make the thousand-foot commute from Shoulder Camp every day. While we could rappel down and jumar back up the ropes left in place below our high point, it was taking too much time out of the day, and too much energy away from moving the high point up. We would have to elevate our home field again and set a camp halfway up the wall.

The only potential location for another camp was at the Pyramids—the blocky mini-towers at the halfway point whose platform tops held small banks of snow. The snow was critical because we could not haul water up from Shoulder Camp—one, because it was heavy, and, two, because it would freeze and there was no way to thaw it in the plastic jugs. Without enough room on the Pyramids to set normal tents, we attached two hanging tents to the wall straddling one of the rock platforms and began hauling up supplies.

We knew we would have to employ the same strategy we had used at Shoulder Camp. To make this new place home, we had to stay here. It was not the most comfortable place we could be, and we looked down with fond regard at Shoulder Camp, where Jeff was left to hold the fort. Those two little tents on that chopped-out ledge had come to feel like a palace. We had risen to that view subliminally, because by no conscious comparison could we say it was the most luxurious place on earth. But after having lived there for so many days, it did seem especially pleasant, and this hanging camp at 19,500 feet felt very austere in comparison.

It also seemed extremely tenuous and exposed. We could stand on the sloping platform, which was the size of a scatter rug, but whenever it was wet and the sun disappeared, the rock turned into a skating rink, and after several near slips off the edge, it was obvious that if we didn't stay roped up all the time (even while we slept), we could easily land on the glacier thousands of feet below. Everything else had to be tied in as well—gear, clothing, supplies, even books and toothbrushes. When we came into Hanging Camp from our high point above, the degree of overhang swept us so far out that we had to jump and swing in on the camp, grabbing at anything to anchor us before we swung back out. We often collided with the hanging tents in this maneuver, knocking them askew on their single anchors and tipping out anything that was loose. It was a long, slow, heart-stopping free fall to the ground, and we became very careful to make sure that nothing *was* loose.

The view from our bedroom door at this elevation was spectacular, but it was also unnerving: row upon row of jagged peaks for sixty miles. We could see down the glacier-filled valleys to where the glaciers ended and all turned brown and blurred into the endless horizon. At night, mortar fire between Pakistan and India over the disputed Kashmir region lit up the distance like soundless heat lightning, and when darkness completely descended, we felt very far away from safety, and very much alone in an alien world.

This was the most extreme hanging camp I had ever occupied, and I had been in some wild places. The fact that it was so far beyond my own experience concerned me, and that concern was reflected in my teammates. We were also worried because the overhanging headwall above us only partly shielded us from rock and ice fall, and we kept looking up tensely, expecting something to hit us. We felt extremely vulnerable to any storm that might hit as well, and we anxiously scanned the horizons for clouds. I began to realize that if we didn't talk these anxieties out, all the logistical benefits we could gain from our new position would be lost to the trepidation we now felt.

27. You can't dodge a rock until it falls.

The higher you get on a mountain, the more you feel exposed to negative things that might happen. But you cannot stay in your tent afraid of a possible storm while the sun is shining. On a clear blue day, you climb like it's clear, matching action to opportunity. Don't let yourself be stopped by your own apprehension. You need to react at each point to the true environment that you are faced with, not an imagined one.

Objective hazards like storms and falling rock often come from out of the blue, and the higher you are on a mountain, the more you feel exposed to the consequences of such adversity. While the law of gravity dictates that rocks will occasionally fall, just as weather patterns generate storms, we are more often stopped by the fear that a rock might fall than by a rock actually falling. But we can't cower under an overhang, seeking shelter from any rock that might fall, *and* climb a mountain. We couldn't hole up in our tents afraid of a storm on a cloudless day and ever expect to reach the summit.

This point was brought home to me by a team from another country attempting an aid ascent up the less steep west side of Trango Tower at the same time we were free climbing the east face. Based at the next glacier over, they were occasional visitors to our Shoulder Camp early on. They had brought a barometer to help them predict when storms were coming, which seemed a prudent tool, but was one we refused to rely on. Every time the needle on their barometer jiggled toward low pressure, they bailed off the mountain and back to their base camp because Himalayan convention told them to retreat whenever a storm came in, then stage back up when the storm ended.

It clouded over and snowed at least one day of every week we were on Trango Tower, and when the snow ended, the other team would wait for the barometer to confirm the storm was over. It took them two days to regain the elevation they had lost, they would get in one day of climbing, and then their barometer would start to drop again and down they would go. Every time they left the arena, they came back as the visiting team, losing any home court advantage, and gasping in the unfamiliar altitude. The team only climbed a thousand feet up the mountain in the fifty days they were there, and they spent so much time going up and down the dangerous gully on their way to safety that they got hit by serious rock fall several times.

They did not believe you could stay high *and* survive a storm. We did not believe you could keep retreating *and* climb this mountain. The storms were no more dangerous at Shoulder Camp than at the lower camps, and were, in fact, less dangerous because of the frequent avalanches below. But to stay high went against convention, and convention always leans toward prudence and excessive caution. The last thing we wanted to be was careless, and we were acutely aware of our exposed position at the Hanging Camp, but when we talked over our concerns, we realized they were all about things that *might* happen, not what was happening now. We could take precautions to minimize our risk, but we could not let ourselves be paralyzed by a phantom menace.

To hide from falling rocks when rocks aren't falling is the definition of ineffective risk management. Climbing a mountain demands upward movement. Bunkering in with layers of insurance precludes movement. If your objective is to climb the mountain, you must move upward never forgetting that a storm might come, while reacting to the true environment you are facing. If a rock isn't falling, there's no reason to get out of its way.

After less than a week at Hanging Camp, it began to feel more like home. We were adapting quicker than expected because we had been through the process at Shoulder Camp. It was simple velocitizing turned up one more notch, and we were getting good at becoming nonchalant in the extreme. But another factor was working in our favor. We had spent so much time looking up at this last, overhanging section of the upper headwall, wondering what the climbing would be like and how we would perform at this extreme altitude—essentially preclimbing the terrain again and again in our minds—that it seemed familiar ground when we reached it for the first time.

That allowed us to enjoy the classic nature of the climbing we found—beautiful overhanging cracks with the high gymnastic difficulty we had trained for, the kind of climbing the experts did not consider the Himalayas an arena for, and the kind we seek out anywhere and everywhere. We found our physical strength was deteriorating at altitude, as expected, but our ability to climb beyond ourselves was increasing to a surprising degree. Each day brought more progress—even rest days were seen as gaining toward the next day's climb. Only ten pitches remained to be climbed, but they looked like some of the hardest on the mountain and we knew it would take time to complete them.

On the twenty-sixth of August, our sixty-day climbing permit expired. We had been forty days on the wall now, and we knew we needed at least two more weeks. Our liaison officer, occupying Base Camp, radioed up that he could grant us two weeks at his own discretion, but that was the limit. Bill and Donna, who had been helping from Base Camp, went back to Islamabad to take care of the details of our extension, which left Bobby with the responsibility of taking photos from now on. Still, we were confident that, barring bad weather, we could finish in time.

A few days later Jeff radioed up in the morning that he was getting lonely by himself at Shoulder Camp, and he thought he might come up and stay with us at Hanging Camp.

"Absolutely not, Jeff. This is no place you should be," we called back.

"Why not?"

"It's scary. It's dangerous. You've never lived in a hanging camp. It's crazy. It's unheard-of. Something like this just isn't done."

"Is that all?"

Bobby, Mike, and I looked at each other, grasping for words that would describe to him what it was like to sleep with two thousand feet of air beneath you. You feel terribly exposed, and you know you should feel that way because look where you are— in a creaking, popping contraption held by one point you keep checking and rechecking, even though you know it is strong enough. One wrong move up here and . . .

Jeff took advantage of our stunned radio silence to call back up. "Move over," he said, and shut his radio off before we could reply. He reached Hanging Camp late that afternoon, hauling a fifty-pound load. He looked around casually at the suspended disorder, lounged back in the hanging tent, tipped his hat for a better look at us, and asked, "What exactly are you afraid of?"

"We're afraid you might fall off, Jeff," we answered, wondering how we would explain that to his parents, his sister, his brother.

"Am I falling now?"

Jeff took over Hanging Camp as he had Shoulder Camp, melting snow and cooking in the hanging stoves fastened to the sheer wall, dropping down and climbing back up to bring supplies. He also led two more moderate pitches, all of which allowed us to focus more intensely on the choreography of the harder rope lengths. We had only eight to go now, and the summit was in sight. We were all excited, and looking forward to the summit day so close to our grasp. On the forty-fifth day on the main wall, Mike dialed a hard 5.12 crack, moving our high point up one more rope length, and he was belaying me on the next pitch when the late-afternoon sun darkened suddenly. "Holy Hell!" Mike yelled up. "We better get off of here."

Hanging by three fingers, I wrenched around, took one look, and started down-climbing as fast as I could. It was like nothing I had ever seen. A wall of black clouds was rolling toward us like a tsunami, washing over the high peaks and swirling through the valleys. Lightning flicked against the cliffsides and the thunder boomed closer and closer. When I cleared the belay, Mike began rappelling down the ropes to Hanging Camp, where Jeff and Bobby were staring with their mouths open, and I followed as quickly as I could. A warm wind hit us first, swirling up the wall, and that was followed by driving sleet as we zipped ourselves into the hanging tents.

The storm had come from the opposite direction of the other storms, and we learned later that it was a freak monsoon from the Bay of Bengal that collided over the Karakorams with hot winds from the Takla Makan desert. It arrived with much more violence than we had seen, but that evening we thought it was just another storm, and we would be fine because we had shelter, food, and water, and we could wait it out like we had done with all the others.

28. There will always be storms on a mountain.

> While you shouldn't hide from a storm that might
> come, you must acknowledge that if you stay on the
> mountain, a storm will come. Not only are storms a
> random event, they are often untimely, roaring in
> when you are most exposed. But a storm does not end
> the climb, it only suspends the climbing. Because you
> knew that a storm could come, you have a what-if
> plan in place to protect yourself. That plan might not
> keep you comfortable, but it has to keep you alive.

You might go on a day hike without getting rained on, but if you
climb mountains, you will encounter storms, and the only question
will be when and how bad? Half of preparation for a storm is understanding that it could happen. It is not negative thinking to prepare for a storm, no matter how many optimists tell you otherwise.
It is positive planning. Put your energy into preparation to be able
to weather the storms that come, not into a debate on whether the
storms will come.

   You shouldn't begin to plan for a storm when it starts to snow.
It is critical to prepare before the storm comes, to develop a what-
if plan for anything you expect to go wrong. One of the decisions
I made before we left the States was to pack enough sleeping bags
for every team member at every camp. We brought sixteen sleeping bags for the climbing team alone, which seemed excessive to
everyone. But I knew that if we were caught by a storm between
camps it would be critical to have all camps stocked with a minimum for survival so we had the choice of places to take shelter.

   It isn't sufficient to make one plan at the beginning. You constantly have to review and revise plans depending on the changing
conditions. Every step you take on the mountain affects your exposure, so the what-if plan always has to be evolving. The plan

doesn't hinder you from climbing effectively, it helps you climb effectively, because you know you have an answer and that allows you to climb right up until the storm begins.

Your degree of preparation has a direct correlation to the consequences of the storm. If you are caught in a shower, all you need is a raincoat. If you are twelve hours away from shelter when a blinding blizzard hits, your backpack had better be well stocked. It is always wise to have a clue what you might be getting into, but on an unclimbed mountain the adversities are as uncertain as the terrain, and harder to prepare for.

The best preparation for a storm is to have weathered storms in the past. That gives you confidence that you can find a way to get through the next storm without an overly defensive bunker mentality. Faced with limited resources, your plan doesn't have to keep you comfortable, but it has to keep you alive until the storm ends so you can climb again.

We thought that since this storm had come in with such force, it would soon blow out again like violent thunderstorms often do. So we drifted off to sleep feeling fairly confident. It wasn't long before we were slapped back awake. The wind was blowing straight up the wall, lifting our hanging tents and slamming them back down on their single anchors. Bobby and I, wedged head to toe in one tight tent, screamed across the gale to Mike and Jeff in the other, to see if they were all right. They screamed something back, and we at least knew they were still there. The tents continued to buck, and we tried different ways to hold them down, but how do you make yourself heavier?

The seams on our tent fly had started to split, and spindrift sifted over us to accumulate on our sleeping bags. One side of the cotlike base tipped up with each gust, and when we leaned that way to level it, the other side tipped, then the whole tent slammed down violently. We put on every piece of clothing we had for fear that at some point we would get tipped out and anything loose would be lost to the night. It was morning before the wind died down, but then the snow increased, sheathing us in a freezing layer of sleet. We leaned out of our tents to chop our hanging stoves out of the ice, made coffee, and pondered our position.

Night in a blizzard was the wrong time to leave a secure position, but now we had the opportunity to go down. The question was, should we? I pointed out that holding our position, and advancing our position, was the one strategy that had got us this far. It might be a short storm, and if we descended to Shoulder Camp we would lose at least two potential days of climbing.

"How much fuel do we have?" Mike asked.

Jeff had been keeping track: "Two, maybe three days' worth." We hadn't stocked Hanging Camp heavily because the summit was in sight.

"Well, even if the storm ends today, and we wait a day for the snow to melt, we'll still be out of fuel," Mike pointed out.

I couldn't argue with the reality of his logic, and we all agreed that the best choice was to go down to Shoulder Camp, which was better supplied. But I did so with some reluctance, forgetting momentarily that where you are is not as important as where you intend to go.

29. If your focus remains on the summit, you can go left or right or even down in order to eventually arrive there.

Fighting adversity to hold your ground is often both personally satisfying and admired by your team, but can only be the right choice if it's the one that eventually leads to the top. If you automatically dig in your heels when conditions are bad, you can use up resources at an accelerated rate without material gain. The best way to go up might be to come down. Don't compromise your destination for the sake of position. Where you are on a mountain means nothing in comparison to where you are going.

When a storm arrives, your first impulse is to get off the mountain to lessen your exposure. Many expeditions follow this impulse with an uncontrolled retreat, abandoning their position in exchange for perceived security. But if you are stuck in a mountain tent with adequate supplies, a storm is a storm no matter where on the mountain you are, and if you descend, you lose the advantage of position, and often that loss cannot easily be recovered.

An inflexibly tenacious team might hold its ground, fighting adversity with the gritty determination that no storm will budge them from their hard-won place. But the team waiting out the storm at an upper camp might be using up resources that cannot be resupplied. If they are still alive when the storm ends, they often must abandon the climb for want of means to go on. Either decision—to stay or to retreat—is not necessarily incorrect, but the basis for making it might be.

Any decision in response to a storm's arrival has to be made in reference to the summit. You are not fighting for where you are, you fight for where you are going. You make the decisions that will best allow you to go up when the storm ends, and every hour or day that passes, you ask yourself, "Is this still the best decision in relation to the summit? Am I still moving toward my destination?"

If the best way to go up is to go down, you don't retreat. Retreat means going backward, which is a change of destination. You descend and regroup, finding the best position to help you to go up again. Where do you have the most resources strategically cached to allow you to weather the storm? Where will you be best placed to climb again when the storm ends? If you decide to hold your ground, is that decision based on obstinacy, wishful thinking, or a careful analysis of your ability to get through the storm in that position?

For us, the only way to continue to go up was to go down, and our ropes were already freezing to the wall when we began the rappel to Shoulder Camp that morning. What was normally a one-hour descent took three hours of exposure to the blizzard now raging. We crawled into our tents, shed our icy clothing, and sank into sleeping bags to try to recover some warmth. It was fortunate we did not delay our decision, because a single hour of "Let's wait and see" would have made the ropes too icy to descend.

We lay restlessly in the tents listening to the rattle of wind-driven snow hour after hour. By early evening the noise of the gale finally started to fade. "It's ending!" I popped my head out of the sleeping bag and sat up, nudging Bobby. "Do you hear that?"

He sat up. "I don't hear anything."

"Exactly. The storm is over!" I exclaimed. I looked at Bobby and he was gasping, trying to suck in air. I suddenly realized that I couldn't breathe either. Our chests were heaving and our eyes grew wide. The storm hadn't ended, it had buried us alive and we were suffocating in a tent sealed by ice, the storm's fury muffled by two feet of wet snow. Frantically, Bobby fought with the frozen zipper to get the door open and started pawing through the snow wearing only his long underwear. I immediately started putting on storm clothing to go out and dig the rest of the tent free. Every forty-five minutes from that point on, day and night, someone had to go out into the blizzard to clear the tents of their deadly ice shells.

It became one of the few chores to break the monotony as two days of blizzard turned to three. We had day-long chess marathons and talked about places we wanted to go—all of them warm. We slept and woke at odd hours, because day was little different from night. We had already read our small library of books and began to reread them, tearing our favorites in half so two of us could read the same book. Whenever the snow stopped, the wind would come up and whirl the loose snow into a bigger blizzard.

Day three raged into four. We kept thinking the next day it would end. One more day tent-bound is bearable if the sun will come out tomorrow. We listened for the lull, looked for stars and a clearing night sky. We started splitting the books into quarters, so we could all read the same book. When we got tired of reading, we talked about things that didn't matter, and things that did. Bobby had lost feeling in his feet, and we discussed that. It wasn't frostbite, or even cold, we decided. He also had a persistent cough that had lasted for weeks. The cough, like his numb feet, must be caused by altitude, we concluded. We had tried earlier to get Bobby to go down to Base Camp to see if his condition would improve, but he wouldn't go.

The sun did not come out the next day, even though we had pinned all of our hopes on just that. It even snowed inside our tents, shedding the rime of frost from our condensed breath every time we bumped the side, sifting uncomfortably into our sleeping bags. The few books that were worth reading a third time were now ripped apart into single chapters and passed miserly between us, and it was excruciating to find that a key chapter had gotten wet and the pages were frozen together.

All of our cooking and melting snow for water had to be done outside in the blizzard, a miserable chore, and it would have been easier just to eat and drink less. But that would have sacrificed our future ability for present comfort. If we were weaker when the storm ended, we wouldn't be able to complete the climb, and we watched each other carefully to make sure no one was slipping further in health.

30. It's not the severity or duration, but how you weather a storm that counts.

A storm is its own mountain and is often the determining factor in a team's success because it can stop all progress toward the summit. Storms require planning, tactics, and discipline to make it through to the end. To still reach the summit, you must react in a way that best preserves your effectiveness to climb when the storm ends.

Experienced mountaineers have told me that storms are the most defining event on an expedition. A storm hits everyone equally, like an ebbing tide drops all ships, but the teams that continue to the summit find a way to keep climbing even when they are forced to stand still. Good climbers who cannot weather storms rarely summit. It isn't, as you would expect, the severity and duration of the storm that decides an expedition's fate. Those factors cannot be adjusted. It is the team's response to, and action during, a storm that makes the difference.

Weathering a storm is not a simple issue of life or death, but a matter of health on a scale that eventually ends in death by the complete absence of health. You are not just concerned with the health of the team members, but the health of the endeavor— the whole expedition's ability to continue to the summit when the storm ends. But even basic actions to maintain health and effectiveness are difficult during a storm. To go out in the blizzard to melt snow for water is an arduous task, and it is easier to simply not drink. But when on an expedition do you need to be most disciplined and effective—when the sun is out and you are winning despite yourself, or when things aren't going well?

In a good economy, everybody seems to rise without even trying hard. But how do you keep rising when a storm comes? By looking for ways to strengthen the elements that allow you to rise. A storm turns the expedition back on itself, and that is a perfect opportunity to refocus, regroup, and recover. Look for ways to gain ground even if you can't climb. A storm might decimate your resources, but it should strengthen your resourcefulness. Companies that weather storms best make decisions that reduce their exposure to the storm while strategically preserving their capacity to climb.

There is a difference between merely surviving a storm, and coming through a storm optimally prepared to climb when it ends. In one case you simply have a heartbeat, and no intention of going back up. In the other you have the maximum amount of health that the storm will allow, with every intention of going back up. The difference lies in thinking beyond this storm's summit—what you want to be capable of and where you intend to go when the storm ends.

Every decision you make during a storm has to have a why attached. Why are you doing this? The reason you go out in the storm to melt snow for water is not to simply stay alive, but to be optimally prepared to go on when the storm ends. The summit is still the immediate and final authority, and when you are deciding on an action (or inaction), ask, "Will this move me toward the summit or am I slipping farther away?"

Contrary to perception, a storm is often not one continuous event. There are pockets of opportunity in every storm to enhance the success of the expedition—a momentary break in the clouds or a fading of the gale. A team or a company should always look for and be poised to move toward such an opportunity because those opportunities are limited. In earlier storms on Trango, we often found an hour or two of clearing skies that allowed us to climb another rope length or haul supplies. If we had simply given up the entire day because it was snowing in the morning, we wouldn't have made it a thousand feet up the mountain.

This latest storm was giving us little opportunity. On the sixth day there was enough of a lull that I tried to go down a thousand feet to Notch Camp to resupply our stock of food, which had started to dwindle, and fuel, which had become so precious we were melting snow in plastic bags brought with us into our sleeping bags. I found the lower ropes frozen to the wall under twelve inches of ice. After chopping out sixty feet in two hours, I was frozen myself and climbed soberly back up with the news that even if we wanted to go down now, we couldn't.

It started snowing again that evening and turned back into a blizzard the next day. We could no longer remember clearly what the sun felt like, or how much bigger than a mountain tent or a white-sheeted ledge the world was, because that world did not exist for us anymore. On day eight of the storm, Mike made a list in his journal to record "Evidence of the Storm" as seen from the inside of a tent:

1. Drips melting down and landing on the page.
2. The cribbage board drawn on my sleeping pad, played with M&Ms.
3. Messages scribbled with markers on the nylon tent walls:

"First with your head then with your heart."

"Never Give a Inch." (A motto as Ken Kesey wrote it in
    Sometimes a Great Notion.)

"You must kick at the darkness until it bleeds daylight."

"Cowboy Up!" (Jeff's contribution.)

"God does not play dice."

"All that is not given is lost."

4. The fact that we, and only we, know how to play Spite
    & Malice with an Uno deck.

5. Everything frozen to the side of the tent.

6. Pitter-patter. Two and a half feet of snow today.

7. The fact that it appears we're in a cloud.

On the ninth day of the storm, in a fit of pique, Mike grabbed
the marker, glared at us to see if we dared try to stop him, and
scribbled in the missing "n" from the Kesey quote in my and
Bobby's tent. It now said, "Never Give an Inch." And on the ninth
day the cook, Ali Khan, radioed up that seven climbers we'd spent
the evening with at Paiju Camp on the trek in had died on K2 in
the storm, two more on other mountains, and a Japanese friend of
ours solo climbing nearby Shipton's Tower was also dead. All the
other expeditions had left, and we were the last climbers still alive
in the entire Karakoram Range. "When," our liaison officer
wanted to know on top of it all, "are you coming down? Your extension is about to expire." We had reached our darkest hour.

31. Momentum is a state of mind.

Momentum is usually defined as a body in motion,
but it is more a desire to move the body and is a precious resource because it is hard to get and harder to
hold. A sense of momentum is absolutely critical, especially to a team standing still. If your thoughts are
all about going up, and your plans are about going

up, and all discussion and internal thinking are about going up, then you can be immobilized and still be going up.

How do you keep momentum when you are no longer moving? If the essentials of physical health are taken care of through discipline and planning, the issue of weathering a storm well becomes a mental one. Without the right mind-set, the best-equipped team can come out of a storm into perfect weather, good climbing, and days of supplies only to go down instead of up.

The darkest hour of a storm, that heavy point where you feel you can't possibly rise back up, can make or break an expedition. Even difficult terrain doesn't embody the terrible opposing force that a storm does, because it pins you in place. You cannot affect what is happening outside, and even though you are not failing, by not being able to try to succeed, you sometimes falter. Many expeditions collapse before they even reach the darkest hour, simply because they see it coming.

When adversity falls outside of the planned game, it makes it easy to resent the storm, to consider yourself a victim of bad luck, to say, "If only this didn't happen I could have . . ." But that line of thinking is detrimental because during a storm your attitude is the only thing you can affect. While a storm isn't part of the mountain, like all adversity it is part of the climb. Once a storm is raging, you cannot wish it away, and if you focus only on the negative implications, you are not able to plan for when the storm ends.

To keep momentum when you are forced to stand still, you must think more about the future than the present, to direct your thoughts with an upward spirit, to focus on what you *can* do, not on what you can't do. Momentum can spiral into a downward force if it isn't carefully directed. It is easier to stop a train from running away than it is to stop a runaway train. So you must guard upward momentum like you guard anything precious, and try to increase your stock whenever there is opportunity to advance the effort.

When you have done everything in a day you can do to prepare for the storm's end, to preserve your upward spirit you often have to project yourself beyond the moment by envisioning other rewarding challenges that this challenge will allow you to achieve. During the storm we talked about places we could go, and things we wanted to do. I fantasized about a climbing trip to Vietnam, where pillars of limestone rise directly out of a calm sea, where there was endless oxygen, warmth, and fresh seafood, with an approach that involved simply stepping off a boat. I planned every detail of that trip as day became night became day without distinction. These were not places we were going when the storm ended, but when the climb ended. The path we constructed to our dreams led through this summit, not in the opposite direction.

We have defined momentum as the desire to rise, the body following the mind, but it is hard to keep momentum without morale, the belief that it's worth going on. You can't carry morale in the Expedition Backpack, but any member of the team can be a morale generator if they understand the forces that deplete morale, and the actions that increase it. We often feel that morale is beyond our control, that we can do nothing about the effect of negative events, when in fact there are conscious strategies to positively counter loss of morale.

On the negative side of the morale equation is a long list of downward-pulling forces: a high level of strain and struggle without much visible gain—you are trying hard, but you don't seem to be getting anywhere. Weariness or exhaustion (basic burnout). Lack of reward or appreciation for the effort contributed. Discomfort. Adversity. Isolation. Forgetting the importance of why you are climbing. All decrease morale and make momentum much harder to direct upward. We often overlook the critical nature of morale, especially in a business context where payment for a job is thought to be incentive enough, but low morale impedes performance even in a dedicated team.

You should always look for opportunities to generate morale by applying opposite forces to counter depletion. If progress is hard to measure, develop a finer scale that shows the amount of gain.

Exhaustion or burnout can be treated with disciplined recovery. Heroic effort should be celebrated, and any contribution rewarded with acknowledgment. Discomfort can be placed on a larger scale of reference, and adversity can often be whittled down with a sense of humor about your situation.

Isolation is one of the more subtle causes of losing morale. Even with two people in a tent, we often felt alone in the storm. So most days we crowded all four of us into one tent in order to reinforce each other. It was like squeezing four people under a picnic table. We were huddled close to the point of physical discomfort, but it increased our comfort mentally when we were all in the same boat. And it gave the added benefit of only having to dig out one tent every forty-five minutes, so we were exposed to the storm half as long.

It also allowed us to reinforce our unified sense of mission. If you forget why it was important to climb this mountain, you cannot continue the climb when the storms ends because you have lost your motivation. If you come out of the storm without a commitment to go on to the summit, you may start back up halfheartedly, but the final push to the summit will require whole-hearted effort.

Remember that a mountain is climbed from the top down, because the first step, and every step you take, is based on taking the last. When things are going well and you can see the summit, it's easy to think that way. In a storm, it is easy to forget. The mantra of every morning to set the tone for the day is a reinforcement of where you are going and why you are going there. Be willing to share with the rest of the team the morale you have generated. Fear and uncertainty are contagious in a crowd, but so are courage and resolve.

We sat through that ninth and darkest day of the storm, four in one tent, and came to realize that our darkest days can be the most illuminating. We were forced to focus on the very elements and inner workings of our beliefs, and to shore up whatever pillars were likely to crumble. Under pressure, the element carbon becomes either coal dust or diamonds. We were being compressed by the terrible pressure of not being able to climb, of facing down the deadliest storm in Karakoram history, of being confined for nine days in a space the size of a table, and we had stopped believing the storm would end tomorrow. I thought back to my winter Gannett expedition, how some of the team never again would go out in the cold, and some of the team never again feared the cold. Coal dust or diamonds . . .

We had been at 18,500 feet or higher for fifty-one straight days now, and away from home for seventy-two. We were thin and ragged. "Hangin' with these bearded men," Mike wrote in his journal. "Jeff with the Russian Elvis sideburns, me and my blond knight look, Bobby with this scant mustache and deep Lincoln beard, and Todd on his way to unrecognizable Grizzly Adams. What will they all think when we get back."

Only seven pitches remained to be climbed above, but the summit seemed farther away by the hour. As night descended that ninth day, we kept postponing our evening radio call. We would have to ask the liaison officer for more time. Even if the storm ended tomorrow, it would take days to pull our camps and equipment off the mountain. Over the crackle of fading batteries we heard the distress in the LO's voice. "You are only allowed three more days," he said. "Everyone else is gone. I will send for your porters." We sat in dark silence, crushed under the weight of all we had been through, faint shadows in the Himalayan night. Finally Mike spoke up, and we could hear the diamond in his voice. "Someone has to tell him that it ain't over till it's over."

7. THE LAST 10 PERCENT

How to Go the Distance When You Would Rather Go Home

After nine days of a heavy, dark, ice-cave existence, on the morning of the tenth day the sun finally rose brilliantly, and the whole world avalanched. Under the warmth of sunlight, the mountain unsheathed itself in an hour and a half with a cascade of ice like an arctic waterfall complete with crashing icebergs. Huge pieces came flying past us as we huddled under the overhang that sheltered our Shoulder Camp. We could look across and see the same thing happening on Great Trango and Biali and Masherbrum—avalanches triggering avalanches from all sides with a shuddering roar that drowned out conversation.

Like moles coming out from underground, we squinted in the unfamiliar light, suspicious of its promise, and uncertain what to do next. As the rock warmed, our ropes were gradually freed from their icy lockdown. We now had the option to go down—we could leave the Hanging Camp and all of our ropes and get the hell out of there. Nobody would have blamed us. Being the only survivors, I think we had validity in the argument of abandoning our gear in favor of our lives. We had come across stashes of old gear on this mountain from expeditions that had done just that, and the highest peaks are littered with such refuse from abandoned climbs.

Or we could take the time to pull our equipment and then go

home. We did not really believe our lives were more in danger now than they had been at any other point, and we wanted to leave the mountain more pristine than we found it, so the gear would have to come down when we did. We could pull it in three days, be home in a week to see people we missed, and enjoy the comforts of central heating, good food, and a soft bed.

It was easy to believe that while the mountain hadn't beaten us—we had yet to find a section of rock that we couldn't work through—the accumulated adversities in the climb had been too much. If the storm hadn't robbed us of the chance to finish when we were so close, if altitude hadn't taken so much more out of us than we expected, if Steve had been able to stay, if we hadn't been detained in Islamabad for ten days when we could have been climbing . . . We had plenty of excuses to convince others and to convince ourselves.

The alternative to that sure path toward security and comfort was to go back up and try to finish what we started, even though there was no guarantee that we could finish. The mountain might still beat us, because the pitches that remained were some of the hardest, and we would arrive there with less of everything material we needed to go on. We had already gained 90 percent of what the mountain had to give us. Was the last 10 percent worth continuing to fight for? Wouldn't it be wiser just to cash in our chips and go home?

If we had spent all our time during the storm wishing we hadn't come, thinking about going home, and planning for our retreat, the decision would already have been made. But we had worked hard during the storm in the only way we could, to preserve our ability and desire to keep climbing, so we had the option to go up when the storm ended. But we still had to act on that option, to take it up or let it go, and the final stretch of any endeavor is weighted with reasons to let it go.

The fatigue of having come so far up the mountain often makes us believe we don't have the stamina to go on. The discomfort of moving into an even more hostile environment makes us wonder if reaching the goal is worth the pain. The pressure of performing at an ever more critical level is daunting. Dwindling resources, including time and morale, make us question if it is possible to reach the summit, and if it looks like we will probably fail, what is the point in continuing to try to succeed?

Like a storm, the final stretch of a great endeavor must be considered its own mountain. You are, in essence, starting the process over again—dealing with the same trepidation and unwillingness to begin, breaking the mountain into manageable parts, replanning your resources, risking failure in order to succeed, falling toward the summit. You must empty your backpack here and sort out what you need from what you don't need to go on.

In some ways you have less to work with now, but in some ways you have more. This is a much smaller mountain than the one you started with. You are a better climber now. And you finally have the opportunity to gain all that the mountain has to give you. Every additional step you now take saves you from retracing the million steps to arrive back at this point to have another opportunity. A mountain climbed to the summit is a mountain that doesn't have to be climbed twice.

32. The greatest gain on a mountain comes not from the first 90 percent, but in finishing the last 10.

> In the last 10 percent of any endeavor, you are asked to do the most with the least resources left. As you approach the summit, you have less strength, fewer supplies, and more hostile conditions. But the same challenge that has taken this toll has made you the climber to finish the mountain. The first stages of the ascent have honed you to the edge of who you were; only the end can forge you into something more.

Because all of the variables—time, resources, energy, environment—will be less in your favor, the final stretch of the mountain will likely be the most difficult part of the climb. If you assume this from the beginning, you will preserve as many resources as you can for the summit push, but it always takes more at the end than you expect. Expectation can be your enemy here if it doesn't match reality, or your friend if you have prepared yourself for whatever you meet. You should expect the end to be hard, so you can start to rise to the occasion before the occasion arises.

To finish the last 10 percent, morale must match the terrain, and knowing from the beginning that it will be hardest at the end brings with it a reserve of fighting spirit to cross the finish line. But because the end is rarely what you had imagined it to be, you often need to recalibrate the team to the reality at hand, to cultivate a rising spirit to meet the rising difficulty. Morale is your most renewable resource and can be generated by reinforcing the validity of the goal, by encouraging your teammates, and by holding to the summit as your compass point. You want to capitalize on the bright energy that comes with the summit push, the realization that performance counts more now, the exciting pull from the end of the goal.

It isn't just your own morale you need to be concerned with at this point, but the whole team's. If one member is drifting from the summit, they can pull others with them. Stress often divides a team, fragmenting common purpose, and causing dissonance in desire. To preserve unified upward momentum, you must reinforce each other, if for no other reason than because it is in your own self-interest for the endeavor to succeed.

So many things are working against you at the end that it is easy to forget the alchemy factor in this foreshortened equation. You may be exhausted, your supply line stretched thin, and the conditions extreme, but the balancing factor is that you have become a better climber in response to the challenge. Climbing the first 90 percent of the mountain is the only process that can set you up for the last 10. You are no longer the same climber you were at the base, and sometimes that is all you have got.

When you come, high on the mountain, to the end of what you were, this is not a point on the journey to be feared, even though you don't know if you can find enough answers to finish. This is the reason to climb mountains. To turn back now is to waste the first 90 percent. Out here you are gaining at a rate that is so accelerated and so precious that each step is worth more than the first 90 percent of another mountain would be.

While the first stages of the climb bring you to the edge of who you were, the end demands that you become more than you were. Crowds can make it quite high up a mountain, but it takes the people who are willing to transcend themselves to be able to go that last 10 percent. Remember that this is the final installment of what the mountain has to give you. If it was worth beginning, it is certainly worth finishing, because the greatest treasures are still to be gained.

When we felt the first sunshine after nine days of storm, it marked the most tenuous balance point we had reached on the expedition. So many teams go down at this point because the residual weight of the storm combines with the weight of the remaining mountain to crush their desire to go back up. During hard times, desire is often the first casualty. Having been extremely uncomfortable under the strain of adversity, it is easy to become risk-averse, to not ever want to put yourself in that position again. You then go back to moderate mountains, or simply quit climbing.

While it is easy to be moderately successful at almost anything, to make breakthroughs you have to get back on the horse that bucked you off. You don't do it to show the horse you've not been beaten, you do it to show yourself. The reason you got on the horse to begin with was because you thought it would be worth the ride. Lying on the ground, you doubt the ride is ever worth the risk. The line between foolish and intrepid might seem to be thinly drawn, but one gets back on to see where he can go, and the other to go where he sees he can.

The storm had dumped us to the ground, and then trampled us beneath its pounding feet, and we got up dazed, but we still wanted to get back on. The logistics to finish the climb did not look positive, though, and despite still having the desire, we did not know if we had the capacity because so much of what we had arrived with was gone. We had long ago used up our wall rations—all the freeze-dried food and white gas for the stoves. During the storm we had tried to conserve food and fuel, eating powdered meal replacement formula that did not require cooking, mixed with snow melted in our sleeping bags. Besides powdered formula and moldy energy bars, all we had left was slow-cooking rice and lentils with no salt or spice.

Our ropes had numerous abrasions in the sheathing, which under normal circumstances would make us discard them as unsafe. Cuts on our hands had failed to heal, and our sunburned ears and lips kept cracking and bleeding. We had all lost so much weight we were starting to look like concentration camp survivors. We were legally out of time, and I wryly wondered if military helicopters would arrive soon to try to shoot us off the mountain. By any formula as to what was rationally possible, it looked doubtful that we could succeed, and if it was likely we couldn't succeed, why bother to try?

33. Don't ask if reaching the summit is possible; ask if it is impossible.

There are many obstacles to finishing a climb, including fatigue, exposure, and lack of resources, but it is rarely the mountain that stops you from climbing it. In a difficult situation, the norm is not to fail, but to give up. Faced with the prospect of failure, many people turn back when they could still reach the summit. They quit before they are stopped because of the potential that they might be stopped. Before you turn back, don't ask if it is possible to finish the climb, because you cannot answer definitively that it is. Ask instead if it is impossible and see how rarely you answer yes.

In the last 10 percent, when all factors are combined, the probability of success often seems exceedingly small. What you do with that realization is a question of whether the glass is almost empty, or a swallow full. Given an uncertain outcome, where the equation of what you have left doesn't seem equal to where you intend to go, if you ask, "Is it possible to do this?" you cannot answer yes with any certainty because you honestly do not know if it is possible. That uncertainty is discouraging and makes you question if it is even worth trying to go on.

But if you ask, "Is it impossible?" you almost always answer, "Well, no. It's not *im*possible," and the door opens to solutions. "If we did this and this and this, then we could move to here, and then we would be in position to move to there . . ." Every additional step you take is a step closer to the summit, and it gives you the option of another step. Discerning the difference between impossible and possible often marks the divide between going to the summit or going home.

When you reach a stage on the climb where it is very difficult to go on, if you have not questioned the impossibility of continuing, it is easy to convince yourself that you have failed, that the mountain has beaten you. But have you actually failed, or are you giving up because of the prospect of failure? Failing is better than giving up on a climb, because it means that you have truly gone as far as you could go.

The obvious outcome of failing and giving up is the same—you do not finish climbing the mountain—so why, you might wonder, does it matter? If you have not actually failed, you could still possibly succeed. Since quitting the climb has immediate and seductive rewards—increased comfort, less struggle, a downhill ride—it is easy to tip in that direction. Your excuses are always defendable: you ran out of time, the weather was uncooperative, you were short on some critical resource, everyone was just too worn out, you had no more desire. And, in truth, if you have not built the foundation solidly to this point with the intention of reaching the summit, it all might crumble beneath you by your own design.

Just as it is easy to turn back at the prospect of failure, it is also easy to make a habit of turning back on every mountain closer and closer to the ground, mistaking uncertainty for actual failure, and defending retreat by claiming defeat. The rewards of turning back have revealed themselves, but are they more valuable than the

rewards of going on? To succeed in future endeavors, it is important to honestly recognize the difference between failing and giving up. In one you went as far as you could; in the other you went
as far as you thought you could.

In climbing, like everything else, there may be in reality a point
where you cannot go farther. If you have tried every conceivable
solution, and you have to answer yes, continuing on is truly impossible, then you have failed. But within that failure is a high degree of success, because it has taken you out to the edge of what
that mountain can give you, which can be applied to other mountains and to your Lifelong Ascent. And if the destination is worth
going to, there can be no such thing as giving up. If you fail on one
attempt, you will have gained the skill, knowledge, and option to
succeed on another attempt.

There is a sense of resolution in failure that allows you to move
on with increased ambition. Imagine how players feel when a contest is called off midgame due to rain. They have neither won nor
lost, only suspended their aspiration. If you call off your own
game, you will feel the same dissatisfied sense of suspension. Failure is at least definitive, and that allows you to take the lessons and
move on. Of course, you would rather succeed—but to be able to
succeed you must stay in the game.

By noon most of the ice had quit falling off Trango Tower, and
we were poised on the brink. We had asked ourselves if it was possible to finish the climb, and we could not answer yes. So many aspects looked doubtful. Then we asked ourselves if it was impossible,
and we also could not answer yes. If it was not impossible, it might
still be possible, but was it worth the risk? Did the mountain still
have something to give us? Each had been in his own private world
during the storm, reviewing why he was here, and what direction he
wanted to go. We had spent as much time together as possible during the day, to reinforce each other's desire, but the nights had been
long, often sleepless, and full of doubt.

While we could most likely recover from a wrong decision now,
we could not recover from indecision. Time was our friend only if
we saw how precious it was and used it accordingly. I looked at

Mike standing below the main wall, and he was looking up. I looked at Bobby, and he and his stubborn persistence had never looked anywhere but up. I looked at Jeff and he was looking at me. He was going wherever we were going, and who was going to stop him? If we had ever tried to talk ourselves out of this, we hadn't come close to succeeding.

We called the liaison officer on the radio and said we needed a third extension. Such a thing had never before been granted, he said, but we suspected that such a thing had never before been asked. To get the extension, the LO would have to trek out to Skardu and maybe back to Islamabad and basically beg for it. Even if the answer was no, it would buy us at least ten more days before he could possibly get back to tell us.

We gathered all the fuel and food we had left, and Mike started first across the snowfield, wading through a morass waist deep. Just when he reached the far side, a chunk of ice the size of a room crashed onto the snowfield, obliterating his tracks. He looked back at me with half a smile, like he had won the first round in a game of dodgeball, then started up the ropes unfazed. The rest of us crossed the snowfield one at a time and followed him up the ropes under a shower of ice he dislodged on his way.

The storm had been like a geologic force, wearing on us as the days passed and supplies dwindled, but under the bright sunlight we began to shed that weight, and now felt as buoyant as a continent freed from a glacier. We started laughing at everything—the ice down our necks, the slow pace, the thin air. When we reached Hanging Camp, we imprudently took off our helmets and untied ourselves. We threw important items back and forth as if the ground were two feet away instead of two thousand. It felt more like home now, our native place, than it ever had before. We were not the same team we had been before the storm, we realized, but a new alloy forged under the hammer of extreme adversity. Leave it to the people with small dreams, we thought, to make a big deal out of small problems.

We had plenty of small problems of our own, which had the potential to be big problems. The kerosene we had brought up for fuel would not burn efficiently in the hanging stoves. Mike and Jeff set to work rebuilding the stoves, putting in larger jets to get more than a paltry heat from the poor fuel. Once they were hot, the modified stoves would burn the kerosene, but when they were freezing cold, they would not light. We had one pint of auto gas left, which we had been burning since the white gas ran out, and Jeff came up with the brilliant solution of mixing the gas into the kerosene in a ratio of one to twenty parts of each, which was enough gas to ignite the cold stoves.

We didn't have sufficient fuel to cook the remaining rice and lentils for the hours required at high altitude, so we soaked them in bags with snow overnight in our sleeping bags. We cooked the bland concoction as long as we could afford to, but it never lost its crunchy texture. The powdered meal replacement became our main form of sustenance, and while it was hard to think of it as food, it was the best form of nutrition we could have brought with us. We had packed the powder purely as emergency rations, and since nobody wanted to eat it earlier, we had plenty left now. When we got tired of liquid nutrition, we nibbled around the mold on the energy bars. The wrappers had exploded in the heat of Islamabad months earlier, and we wondered if the gray fuzz that had accumulated on the bars since then was bad for us, but we hadn't died yet.

It was enough to make us dream about food we didn't usually crave, and we each swore we could eat a thirty-inch pizza after consuming two double cheeseburgers, French fries, and a chocolate milkshake all in one sitting. The things you don't have can become a focal point in the last 10 percent, because your life would be much more pleasant if you did have them. More time, more rest, more resources of every kind. It is one more hardship in an already difficult time, and to continue to the summit despite the hardship, you must redirect your focus toward what you do have.

34. Improvisation and adaptability, in the end, can be your most valuable resources.

> Do not reject the possibility of continuing simply because your allocated resources appear insufficient. Never forget that all formulas as to what is rational and what is acceptable are made down on the plains. Think about where you are now, what you have left, and what it will take to make it to the summit. Be willing to stretch the resources you have, modify what you can to fill the gaps, and go without what isn't essential in order to continue the climb.

When you are facing the end of a climb, you are often preoccupied with what you don't have because shortages make the completion of your goal more difficult, and lack of essentials makes it seemingly impossible. You might wish you had saved more of one thing and packed more of another, but if you don't have the option of a resupply, what you are lacking is no longer important. The past is unchangeable, and while you can learn from your mistakes and apply those lessons to your next mountain, if your regrets won't help you now, you must leave them behind. Fall forward toward the future and what you can change.

Improvisation is one of your most valuable resources at the end when other resources are scarce. If your equation says you need x to continue and you have no x, can you make x out of y and z? Can you, in reality, get by without x? Can you change the equation to replace x with an equivalent that you do have? Often, the alternative to improvising is quitting the climb. Before you give up, examine what you have to work with, look at what you need, and find a way to make the two coincide.

On the 1970 *Apollo 13* moon mission, when an oxygen tank exploded and disabled the space ship's command module, the three astronauts, Jim Lovell, Jack Swigert, and Fred Haise, as well as the entire NASA team, had to either improvise or lose everything. NASA had contingency plans (a "what-if" scenario) for almost anything that was likely to go wrong, but not for this. With limited time to solve the problem, and fixed resources to work with, if anyone on the team had refused to believe that a solution could be found, it wouldn't have been found.

With their command module powerless, the three astronauts moved into the attached Lunar Exploration Module to sustain life support and awkwardly pilot the craft. The LEM was designed for two people and two days of use, not the four days required to get the astronauts back to earth. There was sufficient oxygen, but the carbon dioxide filters soon became saturated, and without a quick solution the astronauts would be asphyxiated. An engineer on the ground came up with a way to make the square filters in the command module take the place of the saturated round filters of the LEM using only components that could be found onboard. Following his directions, the astronauts used a plastic bag that held their moon suits, a piece of cardboard from a flight manual, and duct tape to modify the filters.

The problems compounded: the astronauts could not visually navigate because they were surrounded by a cloud of crystallized oxygen spewed out from the damaged ship; the LEM's engines and controls were not designed to propel both modules, and the response intended was not guaranteed by the action taken; a battery exploded, then the helium tank blew; condensation was soaking all the electronics, and vented steam made them drift unexpectedly off course. Each new problem required both an analysis of the causes and consequences, and a new solution to compensate, all within the constraints of limited time and resources.

Admittedly, NASA is in the business of problem solving in extreme environments with an ultimate stake, and they worked around the clock to find a way to get the astronauts back when all factors said they shouldn't be able to succeed. They were doing what they were good at, but under extreme pressure, and it would have been easy for one person in that critical loop to give up and declare it impossible. How much you are willing to improvise depends in part on how much is at stake, what other options you have, and whether you have successfully improvised in the past. But improvisation shouldn't be thought of only as a last resort. It can be a creative extension of problem solving at any stage, because the obvious, traditional, expected answer is not always the best answer when the results are extrapolated out to the summit.

Adaptability is another resource critical in the last 10 percent and often forgotten. The environment at the top of a mountain is hostile beyond your normal experience and is made more extreme by fatigue and the pressures of performance. That combined difficulty makes you question your ability to continue. You suffer more if you don't put that suffering into the context of what you will gain. You are climbing this mountain for a reason, and that reason alone is enough to encourage you to continue the climb.

As I pointed out earlier, levels of discomfort fall on a scale of perception. What seems extreme to one person might feel like luxury to another. In the same vein, what once seemed extreme to you might be comfortable now, and you marvel at the distress you once felt. Adaptation is about both context and belief in your ability to become equal to the challenge—looking at the day in the perspective of the larger expedition, and the expedition in the context of your Lifelong Ascent, then rising toward the farthest point. The end of the climb is often only incrementally more challenging than the rest of the climb, and your spirit can expand to accommodate that margin if you allow it to.

We started climbing again the day after we arrived at Hanging Camp, even though it was clear that the climbing season was over now, as the temperature never again rose above freezing. Our muscles were stiff and unwilling after nine days of disuse, but our aspiration was unstoppable. Mike was a dynamo, as if he had waited all his life for something hard enough to call forth his best effort. He was up first in the frosty mornings to light the stoves and get us all moving. During the day he never stopped looking for ways to advance the effort. The worse the adversity, the higher he rose, carrying us with him. Jeff was having the time of his life, and we never ceased to marvel at how confidently he approached everything new to him, and how insistent he was to contribute to every aspect of the endeavor.

Bobby was still coughing, keeping me up half the night in the rowboatlike hanging tent. He looked haggard, but remained adamant that he was fine, pointing out that he was still breathing, and until he stopped, he wouldn't leave the mountain short of the summit. Even though he still lacked feeling in his feet, he willed his way up a hard 5.12 dihedral after working on it for a day and a half. The weather had been steadily going to pieces, with snow squalls blowing through almost daily. A month ago we would have considered these conditions impossible to climb in, but after the nine-day storm, this was comparatively nice, and we found ways to adapt.

With the air temperature consistently below freezing, we had tried prewarming our hands inside our coats before we started up, but as our hands got colder and colder as we climbed, they eventually seized up and failed. The only thing we found that worked was to prefreeze them instead of warming them—to hold our hands against the rock until they were completely numb, then tuck them under armpits until we felt the searing pain of the capillaries finally blowing open, and then they would remain warm enough through the entire pitch. Our hands had the accumulated cuts and scrapes of nearly two months, failing to heal at this high altitude, and we had to tape them at night just to keep the oozing blood from sticking to our sleeping bags.

Following Bobby's labored success on the dihedral, I led two heart-stopping pitches up a treacherous crack the next day. But every day we climbed took more out of us, and I was beginning to fear we wouldn't have enough strength left. If I had built this mountain, I would have put all the hard climbing at the bottom, where we were freshest, and made the ascent progressively easier as everything else became more difficult. But the mountain had its own plan. On our fifty-eighth day on the wall, I had to face a crack that Mike had scouted and thought might be unclimbable—at 20,100 feet, too thin for fingers, and overhanging the entire way.

My key strategy on all the big walls I had climbed was to break the mountain into rope lengths—conceivable pieces of an inconceivable whole. But when I went up to face the thin, overhanging crack that day, for the first time on this entire wall or any wall I had been on, I couldn't believe in climbing the whole rope length. I thought back to my training on boulders and realized the first ten feet of this pitch were no harder than many boulders I had climbed. I focused only on that ten feet, with fingertips pressed against the crack, and toe tips feeling for tiny crystals, inching upward under the strain of gravity until I could reach a more solid hold and rest.

I then looked up and asked, "Can I climb the next ten feet?" The answer, I believed, was yes. But if I had asked, "Can I climb the next hundred feet?" I would have sagged back on the rope and returned to Wyoming. This kind of climbing was my specialty, and I knew, and the rest of the team knew, that this pitch was up to me. I asked myself for another ten feet and reached a spot on the rock with good holds so I could rest a few seconds. I picked another ten-foot landmark, imagined it to be a boulder, and climbed again.

As I neared the top, I could no longer ask for ten feet. My heart muscle hurt, pounding in my chest without oxygen, and sparks were popping in front of my eyes. I tried for five feet, then I asked if I could move my left hand. I finally got both hands on the ledge that marked the top of the pitch, a more solid hold than I could ever hope for, but I could not pull myself up. I shuffled my hands sideways along the ledge, feeling for a foothold to push myself up, risking a terrible pendulum fall if my grip failed. I finally wedged my foot into another crack and crawled up onto the ledge. I was spent. All the reserves I had been saving were gone, as well as some I didn't believe I had in me. I was too exhausted to even move.

Bobby jumared up the rope I had led, and helped me down to Hanging Camp. It was clear I would be useless for the rest of that day, and probably the next. I sat in the door of the hanging tent, my feet swinging out over two thousand feet of thin air, and wondered about all the decisions that had led me to this far point. I looked at the haunted faces of Mike and Bobby, swinging on the ropes to chip ice for water while Jeff huddled over the hanging stoves trying to coax them into flame.

We had come so far toward success and were so close to failing. I thought about what I had learned that day that could help me tomorrow. The only way I had been able to climb that impossible pitch was to break it into possible parts. To begin, you have to believe you can find a way to finish, and it is easier to gather belief in small parcels.

35. Each mountain is made up of rope lengths, and each rope length is made up of single steps.

A mountain is most intimidating when you view it as one unbroken objective. But a problem as large and complex as a mountain must be segmented into smaller, more solvable problems. In the end, those segments can be further reduced into fractions each of which has an answer. You trained in elemental movements on boulders to stack into a mountain, and now you can divide your mountain back into boulders, and the boulders back into the elements.

How do you eat an elephant? That is the question that often stands in front of a seemingly insurmountable task. Everybody knows the allegorical answer: one bite at a time. In reality, you have to skin it, cut it into pieces, remove the bones, slice the meat into chunks, stew it for four days, and invite everyone in a hundred-mile radius to eat it before it spoils. But the lesson holds true: the overwhelming task must be reduced to believable and achievable parcels.

When an elephant is standing right in front of you, it's huge. You see that something is too much, and if you can't as a whole believe in it mentally, the body follows the mind. You have to find a way to gain momentum in your mind so the body will follow. To begin climbing the mountain, you had to break it down into conceivable parts; to finish the mountain, you often have to break it down into even smaller parts.

Reducing the complexity of the question to guarantee a yes answer is a useful strategy in a desperate place. You break the objective down by choosing reachable and recognizable landmarks to move to. Each point then becomes its own summit, the microfocus of your effort. Marathon runners often use this technique, choosing a corner to run to, then a tree—each interval easily within their proven ability, and the single goal they concentrate on.

In climbing, we train our elemental movements on short pieces of rock or boulders, to then stack into mountains. On mountains we climb rope-length pitches, and when the difficulty is extreme, we divide the pitches into boulders, and the boulders into the elements of one hand pulling up, then another. The key is to frame the problem concisely enough so that when you ask yourself, "Can I do this?" the answer is always "Yes, this I can do."

Breaking the impossible task into possible parts is an accessible approach to overwhelming problem solving, and you might wonder why people don't apply it more often to relieve the stress and frustration of overload. As in most things that are fundamental, they're not lessons that you don't know; they are lessons you forget. When they are most important is when they are most often forgotten. Out on the plains, it is easy to be calm and logical. But the stress of proximity makes logical thinking more difficult. If you take two steps back, the elephant isn't as big. Solutions are often found by changing the scale of the problem, zooming in or out to focus on either the forest or the trees.

As the Himalayan night closed in with its cold and hostile embrace, we realized that we had to employ any and every strategy we could now, for winter had clearly arrived in the Karakoram, and we could no longer assume that we would have a second chance. Another big storm would literally finish us off, and we knew we were climbing on borrowed time. We had one difficult pitch remaining, the last obstacle to be overcome on the climb, with only wallowy snow to the summit above, and we all went up the next morning with both anticipation and unease.

It was Bobby's pitch, a double crack leading up from the ledge I had reached the day before, and Bobby knew how important it was to succeed on his first try, because he wouldn't have enough strength left to try again. He stood looking up at it, then sat and looked out into space. The cold gray sky started spitting snow.

We huddled together, trying to bolster Bobby's confidence. He placed his hands on the rock to prefreeze them, and we watched as he tucked them inside his coat, looking for the agonized eye roll that said he was ready. Mike settled in to a belay position, and Bobby started up, climbing worse than I had ever seen him climb, clinging fiercely to each hold, uncharacteristically lunging and flailing, staying on, it appeared, by sheer will alone.

We watched with concern as he passed up opportunities to place protective gear to clip into, running the rope out farther and farther, concentrating only on not falling. Bobby had never been good at thinking in terms of self-preservation, and his reputation for being unkillable was no joke, for he had frequently come out unscathed from situations he should never have been in. "Focus, Bobby," we yelled. "Watch what you're doing!" His feet blew off and he was hanging from one hand. He struggled to pull himself back together, got a solid hold on the rock, clipped his rope into a cam he placed, then started up again in an improbable choppy flail.

Higher. Higher. We couldn't believe he was still hanging on. He was now five feet from the top, and we were wildly yelling encouragement. *He's going to make it!* we thought. The mountain was ours. Only five feet left of three thousand, after fifty-nine days, the last living climbers in the Karakoram, and we were about to succeed. Without warning, without any indication that he knew he was coming off, Bobby came screaming through the air in a forty-foot fall and a shower of blood. Mike was yanked up from his belay and slammed into the wall as Bobby hit the end of the rope and swung back and forth sixty feet above our heads.

Mike lowered him down. We looked at Bobby's bleeding hand, and he'd ripped a big flap off his left ring finger on the sharp rock when he slipped. Bobby was gibbering incoherently, and the snow-covered ledge was spattered with frozen red drops. We couldn't speak, silent in the momentous realization that we had come so far, and we could go no farther. If Bobby was healthy and fresh and hadn't nearly torn his fingertip off, he could and would try again. But not now.

This is it, I thought, *the mountain has finally beaten us.*

We had run out of opportunities. I knew I didn't have the reserves left to do this pitch, not now, not tomorrow. Mike had worn himself out doing everything else. It was too technically difficult for Jeff to succeed on. We were done. I tried to say something like "Well, we gave it our best try," but I could not make the words come out. We stood looking down at the stained snow. Bobby was finally calming down, and we got him to hold pressure on his finger to stop the bleeding.

"I was thinking all wrong," he said. "I wasn't trying to succeed, I was trying to not fail." He was shaking his head in disbelief. How could it all come down to this? We tried to console him. Anything could have stopped us. Just because he was the last up to bat didn't mean he was the one who lost the game. We had all failed, because none of us could any longer move the team toward success. Bobby sat down with his back to the rock and his head between his knees, the very picture of defeat. The rest of us waited for him to recover enough to go down for the last time.

The sky darkened, and the snow swirled more heavily around us. Bobby still sat, holding his damaged finger. The snow was growing drifts on his jacket. None of us would look at the others, shoring up our own torn worlds. It was now late in the afternoon, and Bobby finally stood up. He looked at us and said the last thing we expected to hear. "If you tape me up, I think I can give it another try."

36. If you can take one step, you can take one more.

The real magic in climbing is to reach the edge of all you have known, to be at the failing point of strength and courage, and yet still be drawn another step toward the summit. You don't have to ask yourself, "Can I climb another mountain?" or "Can I run another marathon?" You ask yourself at that point, "Can I take one more step?" It is human nature to always answer yes.

In any endeavor—a business project, a sales quarter, or a mountain climb—the hardest steps are often the last, but they also offer the greatest opportunity for gain. The immediate benefit of saying yes to one more step up the mountain is that it gives you the option of continuing. If there is a single no, a mountain made up of ten million steps will not be climbed. There are many forces working against those final steps, and one of the most powerful is exhaustion. You have come so far and it has taken so much to get here that even one more step feels like too much to ask. But imagine if you suddenly developed amnesia—you might still feel tired, but you wouldn't know that you should feel tired, and the weight of all your past effort would disappear with your memory of past effort. You would then shrug off fatigue as a momentary inconvenience instead of an anchor you are dragging behind you.

Amnesia is not a solution you can apply selectively and at will, you might think, but we often use a technique in climbing where we stop, close our eyes, breathe out definitively, and then focus above, all in a split second. The purpose is to drop the weight of the climbing below us and think only about what is above us. On an expedition, the accumulated weight of fatigue has arrived there stealthily, sneaking in a little more each day, and because you did not intentionally load it into your pack, you may not realize you are carrying it. To take the last steps, you must consciously empty the accumulated sense of fatigue out of your backpack.

You always have a feedback loop running to monitor your external and internal situation, and most of the time that loop runs by itself and feeds you whatever messages you are keyed to hear: if you feel like you should be tired, and you replay again and again how hard you had to work to get here, your loop will tell you that you are tired, and every time it spins around you are more tired. You can consciously control that feedback loop by inserting messages you want to hear, good or bad. *I can't do this* spins around and reinforces that message just as solidly as thinking *No problem*. If you use the feedback loop to reinforce positive messages, you might not be able to alleviate fatigue in the body, but you can eliminate the weight of that fatigue in the mind that controls the body.

Remember that the most difficult step on the ascent is also the point where you are most likely to reverse the order of the Trinity of Ascent, to focus not on where you are going and why you are going there, but to fixate on how bad you feel on that day and make decisions according to your immediate level of discomfort. Those decisions almost always lead downward, and while discomfort is only temporary, the movement away from discomfort can become a lifelong habit rewarded in the short term, but limiting and filled with disappointment in the end.

We are all lucky that one of the assets of human nature is the ability to raise our level of belief. Can we become better? Can we take one more step? That utopian view that improvement should accompany the future is our greatest salvation. The fact that improvement only comes with effort is our greatest obstacle, but the larger the obstacle the greater our gain.

The spirit to finish the mountain is in all of us, but to summon it, we must recall why we are there. It is extremely important at this point to remember and recognize and reinforce the validity of your effort. You want to focus on the micro, but always in reference to the macro. You are not up there to take one more step, you are there to take one more step to climb the mountain. Take out your photo of the mountain as seen from the plains and revisit your dream with the mind-set that conceived it.

The most daring achievement on a mountain is to bring yourself to the edge of what you know to be possible, then ask yourself, "Can I take another step?" To answer yes is to leave the past behind, and to step into the future. To truly gain on your ascent, make the climb stop you, but never stop climbing.

8. THE VIEW FROM THE SUMMIT

What to Look for When
You Are Standing on Top

We pulled out tape and superglue from the equipment pack and went to work on Bobby's finger. We had found the glue to be an unorthodox but effective solution for piecing skin back together, and we had packed enough white athletic tape to plaster the whole mountain. Bobby's hands were a scabbed-over mess, as were all of ours, and in between each deep breath he took to load up on oxygen, he coughed that same gurgling cough we had heard for a month. He stood in drifting flakes of snow looking up at the pitch, gathering himself, sorting in his mind what was important to remember, and what he had to forget. We were all depending on him—he was the one with the three-point shot and two seconds remaining on the clock—but we did not even seem to exist. The weight of expectation alone can make you fail, and Bobby wanted no more of it.

None of us really expected him to succeed now, but we also hadn't expected him to try. I'd never been prouder of my team than when Bobby Model started up the wall that last time. If you took Bobby at that moment and distilled him chemically, analyzed him, and then compared him to the challenge, he was not equal to it. But he left the belay point anyway and started up the double cracks. He was climbing serenely, almost weightless, left hand wedged in the left crack, right hand wedged into the right crack, the toes of his climbing shoes jammed into the narrow space, pulling himself up. Release the left hand, wedge it back in higher up, adjust the feet, pull up. Right hand up again, then left. Stop and place protection, clip the rope in. Right hand up, then left in an elegant vertical ballet.

We watched with intense silence, afraid to break his concentration. He reached the point where the double cracks came together, which required a change of balance. He made the change somewhat awkwardly and moved through it, but now he was beginning to shake, a sure sign that his muscles were stressed to the point of near failure. He reached the crux, and we were sure he would stop and put in more protection, because this was the point he had fallen from last time, and if he fell now, he would land on top of us. But he did not stop.

Relying solely on his unbreakable will, he powered through the crux. We were terrified. He had less than five feet to go, but he was flailing now. We all started screaming encouragement. "You can make it! Focus, Bobby. You've got it!" He swung a hand up and caught the last hold, then got his other hand up. "Hang on!" we yelled. His feet had blown loose, and he was kicking and wriggling in a weak, seventh-grade pull-up. "Come on, Bobby. Pull!" He got his chin even with his hands, and hung there, shaking uncontrollably. Finally, he swung his right leg up and hooked a heel on the ledge, pulling himself up sideways, then rolling up onto the ledge with a triumphant shout. We started cheering wildly, jumping around on our small, snowy ledge and slapping each other on the back.

The outlook had changed from such darkness to so much light in such a short time that our euphoria was ten times more amplified than if Bobby had succeeded on his first try. In that dark moment of suspected failure I had thought, *This is what climbing is about, coming at last to the edge of what you can do.* And that edge, finally reached, was a revelation to me, because I had never been there before. But now I realized that climbing is about going to the edge of what you can do, then going beyond. It is the step you did not think you could take that most illuminates the path ahead.

On the sixtieth day on the main wall, our eighty-first away from home, we climbed on to the summit of Trango Tower. Bobby had completed the real end of the climb the day before, and only snow and ice pitches remained above, which Mike led us up under a clearing sky. We did not need to stand on the geographical summit of Trango, because we had finished the challenge that brought us here, but we wanted to see the view. The climber René Dumonde once said, "You cannot stay on the summit forever. You have to come down again, so why bother in the first place? Simply this: what is above knows what is below, but what is below does not know what is above."

The summit was a thirty-by-thirty-foot platform of snow, like the turret of a castle. We set our video camera up on a tripod to record the moment, each taking turns speaking into it.

"We're really glad to be here after months of trying," I pronounced. "I thought a couple of times that we wouldn't make it. But we pulled together to reach this point, and what really matters is that the journey to get here was magnificent. So many people helped us along the way, and we couldn't have taken the first step or the last without them."

"I can't think of three greater guys to summit a twenty-thousand-five-hundred-foot peak with," Mike said in turn. "The work, the sheer fight of everything we've been doing—most people would have given up. I probably would have given up in the company of most people. But the spirit of this team has put us up to the very top."

Bobby stood up. "Whew," he said. "It's good to be alive."

Jeff took his turn. "I want to donate this climb—"

"You mean dedicate," Mike interrupted.

"Yeah. I want to dedicate this climb to the great state of Wyoming. I only wish my brother Steve was here . . ." It had to be the icy wind that was bringing tears to his eyes, and he wiped them away with his coat sleeve. "But in a way he is here, because I'm here."

37. The summit is made up of all the shoulders you stand upon.

You never arrive at the summit alone. With you are your teammates who shared your struggle and fought for every inch of ground gained. But you also bring the heroes who inspired you, the mentors who took the time to teach you, your supporters who helped to get you there. All of their names belong on the summit register, so when you arrive there, you know you will be in good company.

You reach the summit with an overwhelming sense of reverence and gratitude. Even if you arrive there by yourself, you recognize that you were helped along the way because all great journeys have collaborators: people who influenced your direction before you ever began, those who supported your dream, even total strangers who gave counsel or aid on the road.

I knew that if Bobby Model had not risen out of his frozen blood and led that last pitch, if Mike Lilygren had not kept his sense of humor and fighting spirit for sixty straight days, if Jeff Bechtel hadn't become the most misplaced cowboy in Himalayan history, I would have failed. If Steve Bechtel hadn't shared the dream, I might never have come here. If Paul Piana hadn't believed in me as a partner to the impossible . . . The list stretches back to those who gave material and emotional support to the expedition, the porters who not only carried our mountain of gear but also gave us a native way to look at this challenge. Anyone who has contributed to your ascent goes to the summit with you, and it is important to acknowledge their contribution.

By understanding the value of receiving as well as giving support, you will move much further on your Lifelong Ascent. People who refuse to accept or acknowledge the assistance of others never make it as far as they could have, because they don't recognize the value of that assistance. If you won't stop to ask directions because you can't admit you might be lost, you often waste valuable resources wandering around in the dark. If you decline to give directions when someone needs to find the way, you have forfeited the opportunity to be part of their success. When one rises, we all rise. Remember that you can always choose a higher summit if you are willing to expand the definition of your team.

Whenever we watch someone receive an award and thank a long list of the people who helped them, they are acknowledging that even if they are standing alone in the spotlight, it took a valiant team effort to get them there, and they know it. It is easy to analyze failure, but part of the process of analyzing success is recognizing who helped you and how, so you can carry forward the essentials to repeat your success.

It is important to acknowledge the assistance of others and express your gratitude when you are standing on the summit, not only to begin to analyze your success, but because it is part of a ritual of completion that helps define the accomplishment. A summit reached, if not set in stone, is soon lost. Here is the point to finally stop and reflect on what you have done, how you did it, and who contributed to your endeavor. That helps to fix the summit as a true achievement on your Lifelong Ascent and validates the effort it took to arrive there.

Your final gratitude is always to the mountain for being hard enough to change you on the climb. You never arrive at the summit of an ultimate mountain with the sense that you have conquered it. You may have cursed it on the way, shook your fist at the adversities, wished some days to flatten it or chop it in half, but the mountain was always your ally, never your enemy.

Among the shoulders you stand upon to reach the summit are your own, for you have risen above yourself. While we are sometimes told that a difficult challenge will show what we are made of—as if we began life with everything we would ever get, a fixed entity that either has it or doesn't—what a challenge really reveals is what we are capable of, and that capacity is neither preordained nor fixed. The summit offers the clearest perspective to see who we were, and who we are now.

38. At the summit, you can recognize how far you have come.

You are a fundamentally different person at the summit than you were at the base. You have improved your climbing skills, but, more important, your belief in your potential has soared with your accomplishment. From the summit you can see not only where you've been, you can also recognize the person you've become. That transformation is achieved not by standing on the summit, but in the journey to get there.

Your first reaction when you stand on the summit is "Look how far I can see!" The spectacular view from the top is often your most immediate reward on a climb, the memento most indelibly etched in your mind. Even when you go down, if you forget the details of what you saw from the summit, you will remember the feeling of being able to see so clearly.

But before you leave the summit, it is critical to look downward and inward as well, to understand how far you have come. You need to walk away from the mountain with a strong sense of gain, understanding that you are no longer the person who began this climb. Change is often too incremental to notice during the journey, and in many endeavors the magnitude of gain is difficult to measure at the end, and thus hard to mark.

I believe we are drawn to organized sports in part because they have a built-in measuring stick to gauge improvement and the degree of success. A runner has time and distance to measure against. A football team wins or loses by a number of points and is ranked in its league. Statistics cover every aspect in baseball. Even kids' soccer teams keep score, both to have a goal to move toward and to have a gauge to compare their improvement. In business, you may have finished your project, but what besides the fact that you have finished illustrates your new capacity? If your endeavor has no built-in measuring stick, how do you know what you have gained or if you have gained?

Look at the elements you *can* measure. If you have reached the summit of a mountain harder than you have ever climbed, your climbing skill has undoubtedly improved or you would not be standing at that point. Your definition of comfort has changed as well, which means you can reset the scale of what you believe is reasonable. Your problem-solving ability has necessarily been honed, and you have learned to fall forward. All of these elements add up to an increased belief in what you are capable of. Remember that you are measuring yourself not relative to others, but relative to your own potential.

Ultimately, you've got to have confidence in the process, and recognize that climbing a mountain has a spectacular transformative power. Because the mountain was beyond who you were, you had to become more to reach the summit, and it is critical to understand that you *have* gained because that elevated belief increases the gradient of your Lifelong Ascent. You can aspire to more if you think you are capable of more, and that is the greatest reward you will gain from the climb.

At the end of the journey, you want to stock your backpack with the essentials you collected on the way. The airy summit point of your spire may seem dizzyingly high and insubstantial at the moment, but it has become the foundation at the base of your next dream. To build higher, consolidate the pieces of your accomplishment into blocks solidly laid by effort, measured by reflection, and mortared with aspiration.

We stood on the summit of Trango looking down at how far we had come, and thinking about the things that could have stopped us and didn't, and the things that might have killed us, but hadn't yet. An unwitting mistake at any stage of the expedition has the potential to end the climb, which is why it is so important to think from the summit down, to extrapolate the consequences of a decision beyond the immediate and the obvious. We had avoided or climbed across many expedition-stopping crevasses by building flexibility into our planning with what-if scenarios, by improvising when we lacked what we needed, and by simply refusing to let ourselves be turned back.

Of all the things likely to stop you, a careless use of resources is one of the most frequent crevasses that can turn expeditions back short of their goal, and it also has the potential to kill the climbing entity. Companies that believe they have captured a golden goose live extravagantly until the fox steals it away (or the assayer finally determines the eggs are not gold). A climbing camp that is not thoughtfully stocked when a storm stops all movement can become an icy grave. It isn't necessarily the amount of resources you start with that carries you through, but how you use those resources in relation to the summit.

Time is the resource most often squandered, because there is rarely an accountant to keep track of it. Knowledge of, or even a sense of, extra time can be dangerous, because extra time *will* be wasted. This is not necessarily an issue of working more hours, because effort must always be balanced with recovery. It is more an understanding that time is precious, and performance is as important at the beginning of the game as it is at the end. You want the bright energy of the summit push to infuse the entire climb, and often the most effective way to achieve that is to create a sense of urgency by dividing the mountain into more proximate summits, each with its own deadline.

Another potential crevasse is to insufficiently synchronize a team to the mission. We often allow a fair amount of dissonance and dysfunction in a team at the beginning of an expedition, thinking that it takes time to tune them all, and that time is lost to inefficiency. It is better to synchronize the team before the climb begins, to have everyone understand and agree on where you are going and what it is going to take to get there, so you are working in unison from the start. It is all about thinking from the top down, and while it is easier to simply start climbing and worry about crevasses only when you get to them, by that point you might not be able to get beyond them.

The last 10 percent of a mountain comes with its own crevasses, and one of the most surprising is the repelling force the summit can have. Many of the expeditions that fail do so at this point, and while they usually give the expected reasons of bad weather, fatigue, and lack of resources (including time), they rarely admit to meeting psychological fissures at the top of the mountain that they did not look for a way across.

Easing up near the summit is one of those potential gaps. Paul Piana calls it the "have-it-in-the-bag syndrome"—you start to celebrate before you reach the end because the end is in sight. Instead of focusing that celebratory energy on the summit push, your attention goes toward congratulating yourself, and you let up on the throttle anticipating a stop. So at the point where you can least afford it, you have a failure of focus.

With that decrease of effort, concentration, and vigilance, you can lessen your chances of reaching the summit because there is more room for things to go wrong. In a ball game, this is often where the other team gets back in, because they haven't got it in the bag and they are still trying hard to get it. Many climbers die once they begin moving away from the summit exactly because they no longer have that focus point. Don't forget that even if the summit is in sight, you are still in hostile terrain.

Another crevasse near the top of mountains is generated by a climber's reluctance to convert the pursuit of a goal into the attainment of the goal. Their intention is to reach the summit, but they don't quite get there, and that failure seems inexplicable. I've seen this many times on short, difficult rock climbs of a single rope length that require repeated rehearsals to finesse the sequence. A climber works on the route for days, sometimes weeks or months, can finally move through the crux, and then falls inexplicably off an easy hold near the top.

It is clearly a mental failure, not a physical one, but what is its cause? That route has become for them very comfortable terrain, their native ground, with a familiar challenge to come back to. Finishing the climb means they must move on to a new challenge and new terrain, and the resistance to that move, even for someone who is always seeking a challenge, can give the summit a strong repelling force. They often postpone a success within their grasp to be able to continue the pursuit in familiar terrain.

In a larger endeavor, the reluctance to convert the pursuit of a goal into attainment of the goal can be caused by unfamiliarity with success itself. You might assume that everybody wants to be successful, and theoretically they do, especially if they don't have to work hard to get it. But most people are more familiar with the struggle toward success—that is what they are comfortable with, and success itself is a foreign land where they don't speak the language.

When athletes can turn out a world-class performance in practice, but falter in world-class competition, I suspect part of their failure resides in their resistance to cross the frontier line of success. A celebrated success moves us into a different realm, and it is a landscape that many people are uncomfortable in. It asks new questions that we don't necessarily have the answers to. To cross that frontier line, wherever it appears, you have to have confidence in your ability to find the answers. It is, in essence, another mountain, one you have not imagined becoming native on, one you didn't ever expect to climb.

Because the summit can have a repelling force, that is one reason why it is critical to build each mountain into your Lifelong Ascent, so you understand that this mountain is not an end in itself, but a step on the way to a farther destination. Before you get near the summit, both the organization and the individual need to think about where to go next. During the nine-day storm, when we were pinned in our tents and unable to climb, we spent hours and hours thinking and talking about other mountains, about places we wanted to go and things we wanted to do after we had reached this summit. At the time I thought it was a mental flight away from where we were, a pleasant way to pass an unpleasant time.

But it helped us significantly at the end by allowing us to climb through this summit toward endeavors beyond. We had all come to this mountain with nothing else on the horizon. Personal possessions were locked away in storage, nobody had arranged a job to come back to, or made promises to be somewhere. This mountain had become our world, and as we neared the summit, that world, with all its glory and suffering, was about to end. The summit pulls you up the mountain, but the closer you get to that summit, the less pull it has. You always need something beyond the summit—a Point C, your next mountain—to pull you through the end of the climb.

While there are many forces that can keep you from reaching the summit, you also have to understand that once you do reach the summit, there are forces that conspire to stop you from reaching other summits.

39. The summit may be the end of the climb, but it isn't the end of your ascent.

Your arrival at the summit should come with celebration, as well as understanding that the summit isn't the real goal of your climb, but the end of your goal, the final marker of your accomplishment. Be careful not to let that accomplishment stop your continued ascent. You have acquired a new level of skill, performance, and belief, and that acquisition calls for a new application.

Every decision to this point has been made to arrive at the summit, but your goal was not to stand on the summit or you could have taken a helicopter there. Your goal was to become the climber who could reach the summit. The arrival necessitates the journey to get there. You needed a reference point that did not waver—the summit was your North Star, and that is its value. But where, when you have met the hero in yourself, do you go next?

You might feel a sense of letdown on your arrival, because the summit is the smallest point on a mountain you have climbed step by step: at the top there is no more struggle, no test, no further reason for greatness. It is the one point on the mountain where the transformative power is absent. But reaching the summit merits celebration in recognition of your accomplishment. Here is the point to consolidate all you have gained, to congratulate yourself for who you have become, to recognize that you now have more to go on with.

There is a tremendous value to celebration, even if it must be brief, because along with gratitude to those who helped you, it is an essential component of the ritual of completion. You are preparing your backpack for the next mountain, and part of that preparation involves inventorying the contents, polishing your treasures, throwing away the junk that accumulates on journeys, and neatly repacking so you are ready the next time opportunity breaks your door down.

One of the benefits of climbing a great mountain is that it gives you a tremendous sense of accomplishment, but one of the dangers is that it can stop you from seeking another great mountain. There are several factors at the summit working against your continued ascent, including fatigue, a sense of arrival, and the inability to envision another goal. Like the forces that can prevent your arrival at the summit, these factors can keep you from climbing higher, and they must be watched for and consciously overcome in order to go on.

On an ultimate mountain, you battle fatigue from the first step on, because every step requires tremendous effort. You rest when you need to recover, but always in reference to what the summit demands, and by the time you reach the summit, you have accumulated fatigue that requires a longer rest period. You should always build valleys of recovery into your Lifelong Ascent so you don't feel like life is one endless mountain. Remember, you need to regenerate not just your ability to climb, but your desire as well.

It is also important to understand that fatigue comes in different forms. Physical and mental fatigue often require only a short break to recover from, but emotional fatigue—the accumulated feeling of so many days of effort and stress—is harder to shake. Rest alone won't necessarily alleviate emotional fatigue; it has to be consciously dropped. At the summit you load your backpack with what is essential to carry forward, and you must also empty your pack of what is essential to leave behind. Number one on that list is the sense of fatigue that accumulated with your effort. If all you take away from this climb is how hard it was to reach the summit, you cannot climb a higher mountain beyond this summit because you will be carrying too much weight. Think of past effort as an investment, money in the bank that will accumulate interest to be applied to other mountains.

The second factor that can work against your continued ascent is a sense of arrival. As I stated earlier, success itself can be a danger to future success, because if you are standing on top, why go any higher? But ask yourself if this is as high as you *can* go. Your arrival should be a launching pad for future endeavors. If you think, *I have arrived,* you are focusing on the past, while you should be looking forward to who you can become.

A third factor, the inability to envision another goal beyond this summit, is common to people who have pursued a single path to its farthest end. Imagine a medal-winning Olympic pole-vaulter who has reached his highest goal. The opportunities for continuing on that same path are limited. He still wants to climb, but where can he go next? The Trinity of Ascent can help you sort out other paths of value to pursue, and while it may seem daunting to start over on a different kind of mountain, you are not, in fact, starting over. You are starting on. It is not about where the mountain begins, or where it ends, it is about what you carry forward from each mountain that you can apply to the next.

When you stand at the base of a mountain, all you can see is that mountain. The higher you get up the mountain, the more you can see. But the best view of all comes at the summit. It turned out to be a beautiful day at the summit of Trango Tower, the best we had seen in September. The sky was a deep, high-altitude indigo, and we panned the video camera in a 360-degree view. We could see the pointed top of K2, the mighty bulk of Masherbrum, the beautiful ridges of the Gasherbrums, the intriguing spire of Uli Biaho— mountains upon mountains stretching into China, Afghanistan, Kashmir, and Pakistan.

The one mountain we couldn't see clearly was the one we were standing on. In the early years of climbing in the Karakoram, the dagger-shaped Trango Tower was known only as that Nameless Tower on the way to K2, an object of marvel to those moving toward more traditional, pyramid-shaped peaks. In his classic 1977 book, *In the Throne Room of the Mountain Gods,* Galen Rowell described the whole incredible landscape.

> Most modern mountaineers see the peaks of the Karako-ram as the grandest of nature's art forms, thrust into place by the collision of land masses, then sculpted by eternal winds and snows. . . . Many of the world's great peaks are almost completely blanketed with snow and ice. The Karakoram is an exception. Bold rock outlines shine in the sun, and only weaknesses are hidden beneath the snowy blanket.
>
> The names of the important peaks in the Baltoro region have superseded mere identity and gained an aura of mys-tique. K2, Hidden Peak, Broad Peak, Gasherbrum II, Gasherbrum III, Gasherbrum IV, Masherbrum, and Chogolisa are the eight highest. The very words evoke im-ages in the minds of mountaineers who have never seen them. The ultimate mystique is in the name of a slender granite tower of the Trango group, which some consider to be the finest rock pinnacle in the world. It is called Name-less Tower, a name that overtly denies the possibility of symbolizing the tower in a word. The tower remains above names—it is too grand to be compared with a lesser form, too unique to be defined by language, too everlasting to be affixed with the name of a mere mortal.

It would be hard to find a greater mountain than this once-nameless tower, but we stood on the summit and looked. If we had arrived at the top of Trango by helicopter, all the other summits would seem wildly intimidating. But now every low-angle ridge, every snow slope and easy piece of terrain, was invisible. We were looking through new eyes that saw only what was harder than we'd already done, a new challenge for new levels of ability and belief.

40. Look beyond the summit to envision where you can go.

At the top you have a better view than at any other point, and from there you will recognize that your idea of challenge has changed. Imagine your next summit while you can still see clearly from this one, for beyond the summit all the foothills that looked so enormous on the trek to your mountain will seem small. Of the nameless, unclimbed mountains all around you, only the most formidable will stand out against the transformed line of your ascent.

The summit of a mountain is rarely the place we stand and think about our next mountain. Fatigue, the excitement of accomplishment, and a sense of arrival all make it hard to imagine where to go next. But the summit is the best place to envision another mountain, because here you have the truest perspective of how much farther you can go. Once you leave the mountain, you begin to forget what it was you could see, and the longer you stay down on the plains, the less you believe your native home is in the heights.

Before you come down to the distraction of applause and outside demands, before doubt creeps back to undermine your belief, before you think back to the costs and forget the rewards, imagine where you might be able to go. You now have a greater level of skill and confidence that can be applied to greater challenges. You are not going down, you are going on. You have seen what you are capable of, and that vision is a filter that cleans away choices that are now below you.

You won't necessarily choose your next mountain from this summit, because all of your opportunities aren't visible here. The real question at the summit is not "Where *do* we go from here?" but "Where *can* we go from here?" You have an unparalleled view of what is possible, and that is the viewpoint you want to carry forward. If you had another mountain in mind when you climbed this one, here is the point to reevaluate if it still fits, or if you have already climbed past it. You now need to realign the compass of your Lifelong Ascent to a direction that better reflects your new potential.

When you look beyond the summit, you are looking past your present achievement and toward that achievement's application to further your Lifelong Ascent. You don't want to limit your dreams by basing them solely on past achievement, but you do want to acknowledge the power of achievement to expand your dreams. When envisioning your next mountain, don't forget the alchemy factor inherent in the act of climbing. You not only have a true perspective of the terrain at this point, you have direct evidence that a mountain has the power to take you much higher than you thought you could go.

Your potential to rise to the occasion, to become equal to the challenge, needs to be factored in to your next mountain. You don't want to repeat yourself by looking for an equivalent mountain—you want to exceed yourself by looking for a mountain you know is beyond you, and then believe in the power of the ascent to make you equal.

At the summit you look downward and inward at what you have gained, to illuminate those elements most valuable in your ascent, and to recognize what is essential to carry forward. Beyond the summit you look outward and upward into the future. On the horizon you see mountains that might now be possible, and beyond those, mountains that some would believe impossible. Where is it you want to go?

A journey into the unknown reveals more about the traveler than it does the terrain. The map and guidebook you take away from this mountain were not designed so you could follow your own footsteps up the same mountain, but so you could understand the steps to take on future mountains. How do you decide what the next step should be? Should you turn left or right? How do you know which answer is the correct answer? When you have taken your last step, how do you take the next step?

From the summit of Trango Tower, we could see wave upon wave of mountains filling the horizon, and we regretted that we could not climb them all. In the crystal air and brilliant sunlight, the moment sparkled. Fresh snow traced a filigree on the far ridges and smoothed the trackless glaciers at their feet, and we stood there mesmerized.

We had to look beyond the summit to realize that a mountain is just a step on a greater ascent. No single mountain can take us high enough. From this summit we gained insight into the before-unseeable distance, and we recognized ourselves in the future. We were different people than we had been at the base. We could now understand how far we had come, and we began to imagine where we might be able to go. That leap of vision is achieved not by simply standing on the summit, but by answering the challenge inherent in the journey to get there.

INDEX